ART IN PASTRY

EXPRESSIONS

ART IN PASTRY

Recipes and Ideas for Extraordinary Pies and Tarts

Julie Jones

Photography by Andrew Montgomery

KYLE BOOKS

DEDICATION

For my three wonderful
boys, Evan, Oscar & Myles.
A constant source of inspiration,
love and creative sparks.

&

In loving memory of Ged,
forever my shining light.
Truly the best x

An Hachette UK Company
www.hachette.co.uk

First published in Great Britain in 2022 by Kyle Books,
an imprint of Octopus Publishing Group Limited
Carmelite House
50 Victoria Embankment
London EC4Y 0DZ
www.kylebooks.co.uk

ISBN 978 191 4239137

Distributed in the US by Hachette Book Group, 1290 Avenue
of the Americas, 4th and 5th Floors, New York, NY 10104

Distributed in Canada by Canadian Manda Group,
664 Annette Street, Toronto, Ontario, Canada M6S 2C8

Publisher Joanna Copestick
Editor Tara O'Sullivan
Design Rachel Cross
Food styling Julie Jones
Photographer Andrew Montgomery
Background artwork Rag Arts, www.ragarts.co.uk
Production Emily Noto

Printed and bound in China

10 9 8 7 6 5 4 3 2 1

CONTENTS

Introduction

This isn't a cookbook; it is a book of creativity through food. A book of delicious recipes yes, but also a book of endless pastry faffing, creative freedom and inspiration.

Writing this book, and being given the opportunity to soak up design inspiration in the world around me has been nothing short of a privilege. The days spent researching forced me to stop, look around and see things with new eyes, sometimes noticing things for the first time even though I may have walked past them hundreds of times before. I have seen detail everywhere; I have appreciated art like never before. I have read others' words and verse attentively, listened to conversations and music more intently. I have seen beauty in the most unexpected places. In short, I have thoroughly enjoyed the gifts of others. When people create and are open to sharing their passion, we should absorb it with gratitude. Take it all in, be inspired, then allow our own creativity to flow. Being creative and allowing ourselves time to create is such a soothing and rewarding pastime and one we should all embrace.

My hope is that this book will encourage creative freedom. The recipes themselves are pretty flexible, once the foundations are in place. Great pastry is of course key, as is a delicious filling and both should be baked and cooked properly for maximum enjoyment, but the seasonings, additions, swaps and alternatives are there for you to build up your own flavour profiles. The styling of each pie or tart is also subject to your own creative perception: even though I have given up to six design examples per recipe, there is nothing to stop you from swapping a design idea from one page and mixing it with another – suddenly you have created your own interpretation. This is in fact exactly what I hope you will do. If you're hungry and need to eat quickly, granted, an intricate butterfly-topped pie is not needed, a simple plain-topped pie or tart is what's best for those occasions. Same recipes, same wonderful flavours, just less faff! Everything has its purpose.

However, I will say this: it is always a good idea to have plenty of time set aside when you want to achieve some of the more intricate designs in this book, but do remember that most things can be broken down into stages, so don't ever be overwhelmed. I create my pie tops on baking paper, and quite often have them in the fridge patiently waiting to be transferred to a base when it needs to be baked and eaten. Remove the stress from the hours you set aside, and be open to your own artistic flair. If things don't go to plan, improvise – take a step away and come back to it later. A peaceful environment is a creative one and when peace and creativity collide, magic happens.

I know without question that we do lead busy lives, myself included, but spending even just a few hours a month doing something artistic will be of huge benefit. I had many years of being really low mentally. I was so down and saddened by stress, worry, emotional trauma and grief that I would go as far as to say that I was (most likely) depressed for ten years, not even knowing it until the colours started to return and the beautiful world around me came back in focus. The silver lining of those darker years was finding my love of pie making and pastry art. Pastry therapy (as I call it) was the one constant thing that guided me through. I'm so thankful for the peace that playing with pastry brought me, and of course for the doors it has opened onto my new happier world. Even now, when I find myself overloaded with worry and doubt, or even when I have an overwhelming job list, I force myself to stop, make pastry, create a pie and use that time to process all the whirling thoughts that are consuming me. The next day those overwhelming thoughts have calmed and everything gets done anyway.

Do remember to seek out new inspiration – when you are out walking don't forget to look up: I often marvel at what is above eye level. Inspiration really is everywhere, in every direction you look, if you allow your eyes to see it. As well as taking in the world around you, enjoy visiting your local library, wander down the aisles of reference books and pick them up randomly, get lost in them for a while. An image, a verse from a poem, a sketch or a design may capture your heart and imagination. I'll be forever grateful to those who are willing to share their heart in the pages of books.

I truly hope that pastry can be as therapeutic to you as it is for me.

Happy faffing!

Julie x

USING THIS BOOK

The following chapters are divided by main ingredient: fruit, dairy, meat and fish and vegetables. Within each chapter there are key recipes with up to six design variations shown, with notes on how each design was achieved and the source of inspiration. Each of the recipes will make enough for either one large round or square pie or tart, or six small individual pies or tarts. See tin sizes on page 9.

SOURCES OF INSPIRATION
Architecture: Ceilings, railings, brickwork and windows
Emotions: Love, hurt, happiness and peace
Jewellery: Earrings, rings, cuffs and necklaces
Nature: Flowers, leaves, feathers and butterflies
Textiles: Tassels, prints, weaves and patterns

Many of my designs use simple printed templates that I find online. These are easy to source, simply search for the specific shape you are looking for. For example, if looking for a feather, image search 'printable feather template'. A huge array of templates will be there to choose from. Select the one you like, print it off, cut it out and use that as the template to cut from rolled pastry.

You could also cut images or shapes from colouring books and use those in the same way, or even use a piece of baking paper to trace an image you like from picture books.

Pastry Know-how

THE BASICS

Rather than repeating individual baking instructions for each of the recipes within this book, I thought it would be more helpful to share a general guide to baking all of the sweet and savoury pies and tarts. Below, I talk you through each stage, helping you to achieve that perfect bake.

BASE

Every beautifully crafted and delicious pie starts with a base. I always blind-bake my pastry cases, whether I am making a pie or a tart. Some bakers don't bother, but I always do: get the foundations right and you're already on to a great thing. For full blind-baking instructions, see page 13.

FILLING

To ensure that the filling is as delicious as it can be, do taste it as you go. Use the best ingredients you can find, and don't be shy about adding your favourite seasonings to boost the flavour. A few herbs, citrus zests, a splash of booze or some aromatic spices will enhance the finished filling. Be as creative and inventive with the extra ingredients as you are with your pastry designs.

Because I use a no-crimp method when making my pies, the consistency of the filling is important. The filling shouldn't be overly wet: if it's too juicy, the excess moisture within the enclosed pie will turn to steam in the oven, and could push off the pie lid as it bakes. For this reason, you'll notice that in my filling recipes, I encourage you to make your sauces thick or to 'reduce that juice'. By doing this, you will not only reduce the amount of liquid in the finished filling, you will also concentrate the flavours. When your filling is the right texture and consistency, minimal steam will be created and your carefully crafted pie lid will stay put during baking – no crimp needed.

STEAM HOLES

With this in mind, let's talk about steam holes. Are they necessary? Not always... and you'll notice that in most of the images in this book, there's not a steam hole in sight. This doesn't always mean that they aren't there, however. Some are carefully hidden, but I only ever use them if I feel they are needed. Or, indeed, if they fit the design. With careful and attentive baking, you can usually get away without poking a whopping great hole in your carefully made pie lids.

Steam holes can also be an annoying escape route for bubbling juices, which can burst through and spoil the finish of the baked pie. If you do use steam holes, this annoyance can be avoided by removing the pie from the oven from time to time during baking. Letting the pie sit at room temperature for a few minutes allows the juices to cool a touch and stop bubbling, which means they remain inside the pie, ensuring your overall bake looks perfect.

EGG WASH

This isn't essential, but it is something I always do to add a lovely glaze and colour to the baked pastry. There are a few points to make, though, if you want an even colour. All you'll need are a bit of care, an artist's brush and the right mix of egg to water. I use the egg yolk only, mixed with a few drops of freshly boiled water. Using the whole egg will result in a streaky finish, so don't be tempted. When brushing on the glaze, load the brush, then unload it. What remains within the bristles will be enough to paint the pastry perfectly and evenly. Do this until the entire design is covered, taking your time so as not to displace any carefully placed pastry pieces.

TIN SIZES & PASTRY QUANTITIES

All of the recipes in this book may be used to create several shapes and sizes of pie or tart, without adapting the ingredients. They also all work with the pastry batches described on pages 10 or 11.

TIN SIZES

I have used three different sizes of tin throughout the book: all are loose-bottomed tart tins, even though I also use them for double-crusted pies (ones with both a base and lid). The tins I use are either a 23cm- (9in-) diameter, 2.5cm- (1in-) deep circular loose-bottomed tart tin, a 23cm- (9in-) diameter, 2.5cm- (1in-) deep square loose-bottomed tart tin, or six 12cm- (4½in-) diameter, 2cm- (¾in-) deep circular tins. I use Silverwood Bakeware, which doesn't require greasing. However, if you are unsure if your tins will stick, you can always grease them as an extra precaution. Beside your tins, further useful baking and decorating equipment is listed on page 206.

SERVING SIZES

The large circular tin will provide up to eight portions, the large square tin will provide up to nine portions and the smaller tins will give one substantial portion each.

SWEET OR SAVOURY TART

For an open tart, use one batch of sweet shortcrust pastry (see page 10) or one batch of savoury shortcrust pastry (see page 11) to line your baking tin or six individual tins. Blind-bake and trim according to the instructions on page 13, then leave the baked case in the tin for filling and finishing. Any excess pastry can

be used for decorative flourishes: simply bake separately at 180°C/160°C fan/350°F/gas mark 4 and place on top of the tart after baking.

SWEET OR SAVOURY PIE

A decorative double-crusted pie will require a minimum of two batches of sweet shortcrust pastry (see page 10) or two batches of savoury shortcrust pastry (see page 11). Use one batch of pastry to line your baking tin. Blind-bake and trim according to the instructions on page 13, then leave the baked case in the tin for filling and finishing. Once the filling is made, follow the instructions on page 14 to create your pastry lid. If you want to make a very flamboyant design, you may prefer to make more pastry so your creativity can flow freely. Any remaining pastry can be frozen or baked as snacks.

Basic Pastry Recipes

SWEET SHORTCRUST PASTRY

Makes 1 batch

230g (8oz) plain flour

125g (4½oz) butter, cold, cut into 1cm (½in) cubes

50g (1¾oz) icing sugar, sifted

pinch of salt (if using unsalted butter, which is preferable)

1 egg yolk

2 tablespoons milk

For the egg wash

1 egg yolk, mixed with a few drops of boiling water

This is such a great pastry to work with, perfect for making all of the beautiful designs you can possibly think of. It handles well, and cuts and shapes well too – but most importantly, it tastes amazing! If baked properly, this pastry will be crisp, yet each bite will melt perfectly in your mouth.

Mix the flour and butter in a stand mixer with a paddle attachment on a medium speed until the butter has been incorporated into the flour and the mixture resembles fine breadcrumbs. Add the icing sugar and salt, if using, and mix for a few seconds before adding the egg yolk and milk.

Continue to mix until a cohesive dough forms – this will only take 30–60 seconds, depending on the mixer. Turn the dough out onto the work surface (there is no need to dust with extra flour) and bring swiftly together with your hands, without overworking.

Lay out a long sheet of clingfilm and place the dough on the lower half. Flatten the dough well with the palms of your hands and then fold the other half of the clingfilm over the top. Roll between the clingfilm briefly, then place in the fridge to rest for at least 30 minutes.

The pastry is now ready to be used for lining a tin or for making a beautiful pie top.

Ingredients do differ the world over, so when looking for a plain flour, look for one with a protein content of around 10 per cent, and buy a European-style rather than American-style butter. I always use medium eggs, with a yolk usually weighing around 15g (½ oz), and please do use measuring spoons for the milk to ensure you measure it accurately.

Both the sweet and savoury shortcrust pastry can be made successfully by hand too, just be careful not to overwork the dough when the egg yolk and milk has been added. It will be easier if you have cold hands, so if you are naturally hot-handed, I would suggest you plunge them into iced water for a couple of minutes before starting.

SAVOURY SHORTCRUST PASTRY

Makes 1 batch

230g (8oz) plain flour

125g (4½oz) butter, cold, cut into 1cm (½in) cubes

pinch of salt

1 egg yolk

2 tablespoons milk

For the egg wash

1 egg yolk, mixed with a few drops of boiling water

This pastry is particularly short, but can be used successfully for decorative pastry work. It is surprising how much the dough will change after a rest: the liquid from the egg yolk and the milk is absorbed by the flour as it rests, giving you a great dough to work with. It will never be as pliable as the sweet version (the icing sugar in that makes the dough softer), which is why you sometimes see a savoury dough that contains a little sugar. I have never needed to add sugar to this recipe, but if you have trouble, it will probably be due to the absorption of the flour. If after resting, the dough seems very hard to roll or is cracking around the edges, lightly spray the surface with water, then rewrap and rest again before rolling.

Mix the flour and butter in a stand mixer with a paddle attachment on medium speed until the butter has been incorporated into the flour and the mixture resembles fine breadcrumbs. Add the salt and mix for a few seconds before adding the egg yolk and milk.

Continue to mix until a cohesive dough forms – this will only take 30–60 seconds, depending on the mixer. Turn the dough out onto the work surface (there is no need to dust with extra flour) and bring swiftly together with your hands, without overworking.

Lay out a long sheet of clingfilm and place the dough on the lower half. Flatten the dough well with the palms of your hands and then fold the other half of the clingfilm over the top. Roll between the clingfilm briefly, then rest for at least 30 minutes at room temperature if using to line a tin, or in the fridge if using for decoration.

The pastry is now ready to be used for lining a tin or for making a beautiful pie top.

Blind-baking

I use the same method of rolling, lining and blind-baking for both the sweet and savoury pastry recipes in this book, although the two pastries do behave quite differently from each other. The savoury requires a bit more patience, perhaps, in that it is harder to manipulate into the tins than the sweet. A little extra care is all that's needed.

Cut out two 35cm square (13¾in square) sheets of baking paper. After the pastry has been rested, roll it out between these sheets, aiming to roll it out evenly until it reaches the edges of the paper. This should ensure it's rolled to about the right thickness. Lift the paper now and then as you work, before replacing it and smoothing it out: this prevents creases from being rolled into the pastry surface. Once rolled, lift off the top layer of paper, then invert the pastry onto the tin before peeling off the other layer of paper. Ease the pastry into the edges of the tin, making sure all of the air underneath has been pushed out. If baking six small cases rather than one large, cut the pastry and baking paper into six sections before transferring to the tins. Trim the pastry using scissors so that there is only about 1cm (½in) of excess pastry above the rim. If you're using a fluted tin, push the pastry into each groove, using either the handle of a spatula or, if your hands are cold enough, a finger. It is important to chill the pastry case well before baking. Give it a minimum of 30 minutes in the fridge, or a 5-minute blast in the freezer.

Place a baking sheet in the oven and preheat the oven to 200°C/180°C fan/400°F/Gas mark 6.

When the pastry case has chilled sufficiently and the oven is up to temperature, scrunch up a piece of baking paper bigger than the tin being used, then un-scrunch it and place it over the top of the pastry, pushing it into the edges. Pour enough baking weights on top of the paper to entirely fill the tin: ceramic beads, dried pulses and rice all work, or you can use a mixture. What is really important is that they are heavy.

Bake for 20 minutes, then spoon out all of the baking weights and remove the paper. Reduce this time to 12 minutes if baking six small cases. The base of the pastry case may still look a little raw towards the centre, which is fine and to be expected. Return the empty pastry case to the oven for a further 5 minutes until all of the rawness has baked out but the colour is still relatively pale.

It is important to check the case for any holes or slight cracks at this point. If any are visible, use the leftover pastry to fill these in carefully.

Once you're happy that any holes or cracks have been patched up, prick the pastry case gently with a fork (without making holes) and then glaze all over with an egg wash (see page 8). Not all of the egg wash will be needed, so keep the rest for the decorative lid. Return to the oven for another 15–20 minutes, or until the pastry case is deep golden, crisp and cooked through. This will be more like 10–12 minutes for six small cases. Don't be alarmed if the overhanging edge seems burned: this will be shaved off and discarded. Allow to cool completely in the tin.

The best way to trim the overhanging edge is to use a vegetable peeler, preferably one with a swivel blade. Use the peeler to gently shave away the pastry until the top of the tin has been exposed. Brush away any crumbs that have fallen inside the pastry case.

The case is now ready to be filled and topped with a beautiful pie lid before baking (see page 17), or used as it is for a tart.

Decorative Pie Lids

CREATING

To ensure a sleek, neat finish and to give you more time to be creative, I suggest you make your designs 'off the pie'. The amount of pastry needed will vary from design to design, but what is important is to have enough to play with. There's nothing more frustrating than running short of pastry mid-flow and having to stop to make more. Therefore, if you're making a decorative double-crusted pie, I suggest making three batches (one for the case, one for the platform and one for the decor) so that you can be sure of having enough. Any leftover pastry will keep for a few days in the fridge or a few weeks in the freezer. If you are anything like me, it won't be in there for long: the meditative nature of faffing with pastry will always be a pull.

When you decide to make a pie top, there are a few things I would suggest you consider.
- Are you feeling relaxed, and do you have plenty of time to just forget the rest of the world and create?
- Is your workspace cool?
- Do you have everything you need to hand (see below)?
- Do you have enough pastry?

Below is a quick list of the equipment you'll want to have ready to go. Further detail is given on page 206.
- baking paper
- cocktail sticks or wooden skewers
- rolling pin
- pasta machine with spaghetti and tagliatelle cutters
- various shaped cutters
- palette knife
- pizza wheel
- ruler
- small kitchen knife
- small artist's brushes

First, you will need to roll out a batch of pastry to create a platform upon which to create your design. Roll this out between two pieces of baking paper, making sure it's even. The thickness of the platform pastry will depend on your final design. If some of the platform is to remain uncovered by any further pastry, don't roll it out too thinly, as it will need to withstand the baking process uncovered. If you intend on fully covering the platform, for example with a parquet or weave design, then roll the platform as thinly as you can, as the decorative layers you are adding on top will make the lid much thicker. Ultimately, you want a pie that is tasty and well-baked as well as beautiful, so do always keep this in mind.

When the pastry has been rolled out, leave it on the bottom sheet of baking paper, then use the tin you're using for your pie to lightly press a mark into the pastry. Do not cut all the way through; you just want a light indentation to show you your working area. Leave a border of about 2cm (¾in) around the outside of this, then trim away the rest– this is all extra pastry to use for decorations!

You are now ready to build the design, so get your favourite tunes on and allow yourself to go off track and follow your instincts: that's when creative magic happens. Of course, it's great to have an inspiration source to guide you, but it's when you put your own original spin on what you are creating that your pie becomes truly special. I've included brief instructions for creating the designs featured throughout the book, and I've explained which tools were used for each, but the important thing is just to create. Remember, if things don't go to plan, just walk away for a moment, take time out. When you return, you can change it – or, if all else fails, just hide the bits you don't like with pastry balls. I do that all the time!

Once you're happy with your design, it needs to be chilled. Slide a baking sheet (or piece of stiff cardboard) underneath the baking paper and place your lid in the fridge for about 30 minutes or in the freezer for about 5 minutes until sufficiently chilled and stiffened before transferring the lid to your pie (see page 17). If you aren't ready to bake yet, your lid could be stored in the fridge for up to 3 days, or in the freezer for up to 2 weeks: just be sure to wrap it well with clingfilm first.

Adding Finishing Detail

Even the most intricate designs can be taken a step further with some extra detailing.
Never stop until you are truly satisfied! Adding extra detail to leaves or placing pastry balls,
discs or tendrils will all make the design more intricate, interesting and unique to you. When
working with very small pieces of pastry, the point of a cocktail stick can be a useful tool
for careful positioning.

TRANSFERRING

When you're ready to bring all the elements together to assemble an actual pie, you will need the pre-baked pastry case, still in its tin and filled to the top (or pretty much) with your chosen filling, making sure it is levelled off nicely. Brush some of the egg wash around the rim, then retrieve the chilled pastry lid from either fridge or freezer.

Remove any clingfilm, but leave the baking paper underneath for now. Place the pie lid on top of the filled base and slowly pull back the baking paper from beneath it. As the pie lid will be stiff from chilling, the pastry will stay rigid and the paper should peel off with ease. As you do so, ensure the positioning of the pie lid is correct: the marked-out border and the decoration within the border should match up with the edges of the tin below.

The pastry lid will be quite stiff depending on how long it has been chilled; if it's too stiff to work with, just leave it sitting on top of the base for a while at room temperature until it starts to soften. When softened, it's time to trim it to neaten the edges: all you need for this is a warm thumb! Use your fingers to judge where the edge of the tin is, then press down with your thumb on the pastry until it meets the rim. When it does, keep pressing with a slight outward and downward motion, and the excess pastry will come away easily. As you press, the lid will seal on to the pastry case below, with the egg wash acting like a glue. Continue all the way around the tin until you have a beautifully neat pie.

The pie is now ready to bake. It is essential that your pastry lid is still cold before baking. Always think: cold pastry, hot oven. Any other way will result in your pastry melting before it has the chance to crisp up, and this means any decorations or detail you've added to your pie could be lost. Instructions for most of the pies shown in this book have a general baking time (see the following), but do check the individual recipe page for any specific guidelines.

BAKING

All the double-crust pies in this book are baked at the same temperature: 200°C/180°C fan/400°F/gas 6. The blind-baking process means that there's no need to preheat a baking sheet for the pie to sit on in the oven.

Personally, I rarely time the baking of my pies. So the timings I suggest serve only as a guide, as the true baking time will differ from oven to oven, home to home and baker to baker. The way in which you have made your pie will also make a difference: from the intricacy of your design to the tins you use. A rough guideline is around 50 minutes for a large pie and 35 minutes for the smaller pies, unless otherwise stated in the individual recipes. As most of the pie fillings are pre-cooked, all that is needed is for the pie to be baked long enough for the pastry to become golden and crisp, and the filling to be heated through sufficiently.

I suggest that you check your pie after a 30-minute initial bake for a larger pie (20 minutes for the smaller pies). By this time, the pastry will be crisp enough for you to open the oven without risk. There's a high chance that parts of your pie top will be colouring more than other parts, especially if your design is partly raised. A simple rotation in the oven will help in some cases, or you could make a foil 'hat' for those raised parts, folding and shaping kitchen foil and placing it loosely over them before baking further. Check again after another 10 minutes, then every 5 minutes after that, until the pie lid is beautifully baked, golden all over and the filling hot. If you wish, you could use a digital probe to check the temperature of the filling. If the pastry is fully cooked but the filling isn't as hot as you'd like, you can cover the pie with foil and bake it for a little longer.

I recommend allowing any pie to cool in its tin for at least 5 minutes before removing and serving. Pastry is then always best eaten as freshly baked as possible so the pastry is as crisp as it should be. Store any leftovers in the fridge, and if reheating do so in the oven rather than a microwave.

Fruit

All the Berries Tart

**Makes 1 large tart
or 6 small tarts**

For the pastry base

1 batch sweet shortcrust
pastry (page 10)

For the crème pâtissière

4 egg yolks

80g (2¾oz) caster sugar

35g (1½oz) plain flour

330ml (11fl oz) full-fat milk

2 teaspoons vanilla bean
paste

For the topping

600g (1lb 5oz) mixed berries

2 tablespoons clear
redcurrant jelly, to glaze
(optional)

fresh herbs or edible flowers
(optional)

Variations and additions

- Add lemon zest to the
  pastry.

- Add orange blossom water
  to the crème pâtissière.

- Add a layer of jam beneath
  the crème pâtissière.

- Change the fruit according
  to what is in season.

This is a dessert to make at the height of summer, when berries are at their
best, bursting with juice and sweet flavour, and there are more of them than
what you know what do to with. I live near a fantastic pick-your-own farm that
grows strawberries, blueberries, raspberries, red currants, blackcurrants and
ruby gooseberries. It's such a fantastic day out: my boys love going to pick the
fruit, hunting for the biggest, juiciest strawberries they can find. Spending
the days that follow using up all that lovely fruit is a highlight of our summer.

The selection of berries you use here really is up to you. However, the greater
the variety, the more pleasing the finished tart will look – and taste. When placing
the fruit upon the crème pâtissière, try to do so without thinking about it too much.
Be free with it, and build up the aesthetic by changing the way the fruit is cut and
positioned. Small tips of flowering herbs make for a wonderful highlight and add
a burst of fragrant flavour.

Line your tin with the pastry and blind-bake and trim according to the instructions
on page 13. Leave the baked pastry case in the tin for filling and finishing.

To make the crème pâtissière, place the egg yolks and 2 tablespoons of the sugar
in a large bowl. Whisk until the mixture is pale and has some volume. Add the flour
and whisk to combine.

In a large saucepan over a medium heat, stir the milk, vanilla and remaining sugar
together, removing the pan from the heat as soon as the mixture boils. Pour a
little of the hot milk over the egg yolks and mix well, then add the remainder while
whisking continuously. Pour the resulting custard back into the pan and bring to a
gentle boil. Allow the custard to bubble and thicken for about 2 minutes, whisking
all the while. Once it has thickened and the raw flour has cooked, transfer the
custard to a bowl, covering the surface with a layer of cling film before it cools to
prevent a skin from forming. Allow to cool completely before use. When you're
ready to assemble the tart, vigorously whisk the chilled mixture until smooth.

Fill the pre-baked pastry case with a layer of the crème pâtissière, saving a small
amount, then level it off, ready for the fruit to be added. Set the remaining crème
pâtissière aside.

continued overleaf

Cut, slice and arrange your chosen berries on top of the crème pâtissière in a loose, creative fashion. Rotate the tart to help you find your flow, then fill in the spaces.

If you want to glaze the tart, gently melt the redcurrant jelly with a splash of water in a small saucepan over a low heat. Don't allow the jelly to boil, as it won't brush easily. Once melted, use a delicate brush to cover the cut fruit with the glaze.

Transfer the reserved crème pâtissière to a piping bag fitted with a small plain nozzle, or use a piping bag with no nozzle. Finish the tart with little dots of crème pâtissière, then add any herbs or edible flowers.

This fruit tart will be best assembled and eaten on the day it was made, as the fruit can begin to look a bit tired after that. That said, if stored in the fridge it will keep for up to 3 days, but it won't look as spectacular as when first made.

All the Berries Pies

**Makes 6 small pies
or 1 large pie**

For the pastry

at least 2 batches sweet
shortcrust pastry (page 10)

For the filling

900g (2lb) mixed berries of
your choice, stalks removed
and larger berries halved

juice of ½ lemon

80g (2¾oz) icing sugar

½ tablespoon cornflour

Variations and additions

- Add vanilla seeds or citrus
  zest to the pastry.

- Add spices, such as vanilla,
  cinnamon or nutmeg to
  the fruit mixture, or try
  adding some fresh herbs
  like basil, rosemary or
  mint.

- Use cherries or
  gooseberries, or add
  some apple pieces.

To make the most of the rich colour of the berries, you may want to try making this pie with an open design, like the small pies pictured opposite, or an open lattice pattern so that the beautiful purple bubbles pop through the gaps. Whichever design you choose, know this: your mouth will explode with the taste of summer, accompanied by the buttery crispness of perfect pastry. I like to serve this pie hot with top-notch vanilla ice cream.

Line six individual baking tins with one batch of the pastry and blind-bake and trim according to the instructions on page 13. Leave the baked pastry cases in the tins for filling and finishing.

Tip your chosen berries into a large bowl. Squeeze in the lemon juice and stir through the icing sugar, then leave to macerate for up to 2 hours at room temperature. As the fruit macerates, the flavours will be enhanced and the juice will start to run.

After 2 hours, strain the fruit in a sieve, catching the juice in a small saucepan. The juice has so much flavour and shouldn't be wasted, but it needs to be thickened to prevent soggy pastry. Place the saucepan over a medium heat and reduce until the juice thickens into a fruity sauce. Allow to cool before mixing with the drained fruit, and stir through the cornflour.

Fill the pre-baked pastry cases with the fruit and level off neatly.

Top with your decorative pastry lids of choice and bake, following the instructions on page 17.

Tudor Rose

This design uses three circle sizes: large, medium and small. The larger circle has a cut-out of three petals made using a daisy cutter – so simple but very effective. Lay the cut-out circles across the top of the fruit, then brush with egg wash and bake until golden.

Honesty Wreath

This pie was a true expression of emotion when I was making it. Although you would think that the honesty seed was the inspiration, it was actually the lack of honesty I had received that was the true inspiration for making this pie. Inspiration shouldn't only come from physical things; it can be drawn from your emotions too. Expressing your emotions in any art form will probably result in some of your best work.

Cut out a selection of large, medium and small circles from rolled-out pastry. Pull each one slightly to elongate. On a pastry platform, mark out the working area (see page 14), then within that area, use a circular cutter to mark a circle in the middle. Mark a larger circle around that. Build up the wreath using the pastry cut-outs, by placing them around the outer circle, working your way in. Use sugar sprinkles to add stems to each 'seed pod', then indent each twice on either side. Paint with silver edible glitter, then use edible brown paint to gently brush around the edge of each pod, and in the indented grooves.

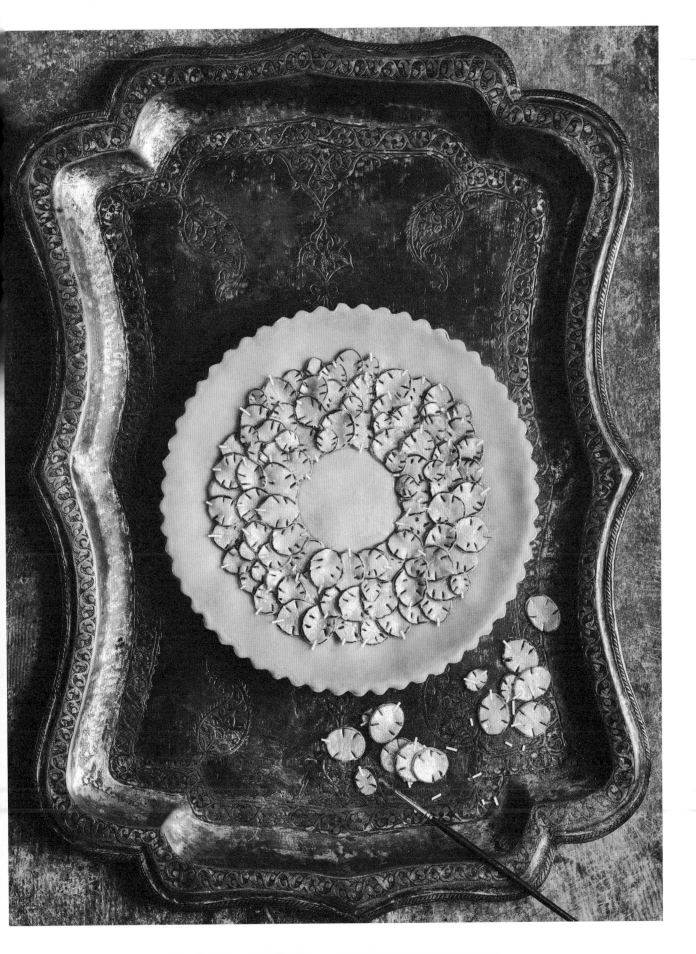

Apple Tart

**Makes 1 large tart
or 6 small tarts**

For the pastry base

1 batch sweet shortcrust
pastry (page 10)

For the frangipane

80g (2¾oz) unsalted butter,
at room temperature

80g (2¾oz) caster sugar,
plus extra for sprinkling

80g (2¾oz) ground almonds

80g (2¾oz) beaten egg

For the topping

1kg (2lb 4oz) eating apples,
ideally with different-
coloured skins

juice of 2 lemons

50g (1¾oz) berries
or currants, such as
blackberries, blueberries or
blackcurrants (optional)

50g (1¾oz) red and green
seedless grapes (optional)

edible glitter (optional)

Variations and additions

- Add spices to the
frangipane, or replace
the butter with cooled
browned butter for extra
flavour.

- Use ground hazelnuts
or walnuts instead of
almonds.

- Spread a layer of jam
beneath the frangipane.

My love of flowers often crosses over into my decorative baking: you only have to flick through this book to see that floral motifs feature heavily in my designs, from dahlias to lupins, lily of the valley to wisteria. Here, I've shared an edible rose garden made of blanched and rolled apple slices, nestled into buttery almond cream.

I haven't given instructions for positioning the 'roses' or the other fruit, as these tarts will never – and should never – be identical. Be free in your placement and just go with it; see what appears, and build the 'garden' flower by flower. Use contrasting fruits to add colour and extra flavour pops. Pastry leaves and shapes will add another dimension, and can be highlighted with edible glitter. Put your favourite playlist on and be an artist for the day.

Line your baking tin with the pastry and blind-bake and trim according to the instructions on page 13. Leave the baked pastry case in the tin for filling and finishing.

To make the frangipane, place the butter and caster sugar in a bowl or stand mixer and beat to combine. Try not to incorporate too much air, as you don't want the frangipane to puff up too much during baking, or it might envelop the apples. Add a third of the ground almonds and mix, then add a splash of the beaten egg and combine. Continue in this manner until all the ground almonds and egg have been added and everything is well combined. Transfer to the fridge to stiffen, while you prepare the apples.

Heat a large saucepan of water over a medium heat and bring to a simmer, then reduce the heat to very low. Place a large bowl of cold water on the side – add some ice, if you have any. Pour half the lemon juice into the pan of warm water and the rest into the bowl of cold water.

Use an apple corer to remove the core from 4 of the apples, then cut each apple in half vertically. Using either a very sharp knife or a mandoline, cut each apple half horizontally into 2mm (⅛in) half-moon slices. Try to keep your slices as consistent as possible, as this will ensure they blanch evenly and give you a neater finish. Plunge the apple slices into the simmering water. The hot water will soften the slices after 30 seconds or so. You want them to become pliable enough to roll without breaking, so test for this regularly. Once they're ready, remove the apple

continued overleaf

slices from the hot water using a slotted spoon and transfer to the cold water to prevent them from softening further. Repeat this process with as many apples as needed: only prepare more when you have used up the first batch to prevent the apple slices from browning.

Cover the base of your pre-baked pastry case with the frangipane and level off with a palette knife or similar.

To make the apple roses, lay out a clean tea towel on the work surface in front of you. Arrange 6–8 apple slices side by side on the tea towel, skin-side facing away from you. The slices must overlap by half each time. Use the corner of the cloth to blot off any excess water from the slices, then, starting with the first apple slice that was laid, roll them up tightly (using both hands is easiest). Place the rolled slices into the frangipane skin-side up: this will hold the apple rose in place. Continue until the entire surface is covered. Add some berries, grapes and unbaked pastry leaves if desired. For a final touch, you can sprinkle on some edible glitter. Place the tart in the fridge for at least an hour.

Preheat the oven to 160°C/140°F fan/325°F/gas mark 3 and place a baking sheet in the oven.

Sprinkle the entire surface of the tart with a fine dusting of caster sugar before covering loosely with tin foil. The tart can take up to 2 hours to bake, depending on how many apples roses have been placed. I suggest checking after the first hour, then every 20 minutes thereafter, removing the foil for the final 20 minutes. The tart is ready when the fruit has softened and you can see that the frangipane has a sponge-like appearance.

Once baked, remove from the oven and allow to cool before removing from the tin.

This tart is best served on the day of baking; however it will keep in the fridge for 3 days. If you want to reheat it, cover with foil and put in the oven at the same temperature for 15–20 minutes. You can also assemble the tart prior to baking.

Apple Roses & Leaves

Roses are one of my favourite garden flowers, from the nude blush pinks to the vibrant oranges and reds, and the small buds of rambling or climbing roses to the big David Austin blowsy show-offs – each variety has its own form of beauty. Take inspiration from the variety of roses when preparing and shaping your apple roses. Use apples with different-coloured skins and vary the size of roses that you make.

Apple Pies

**Makes 6 small pies
or 1 large pie**

For the pastry base

at least 2 batches sweet
shortcrust pastry (page 10)

For the apple filling

50g (1¾oz) soft light brown
sugar

1½ teaspoons ground
cinnamon

pinch of sea salt flakes

60g (2oz) unsalted butter

650g (1lb 7oz) mixed apples,
both cookers and eaters,
peeled, cored and chopped
into 1cm (½in) dice

70g (2½oz) berries or
currants, such as
blackberries, blueberries
or blackcurrants

For the frangipane

30g (1oz) unsalted butter at
room temperature

30g (1oz) caster sugar

30g (1oz) ground almonds

30g (1oz) beaten egg

Variations and additions

- Add vanilla seeds or
  clementine zest to the
  pastry before baking.

- Add fragrant herbs, like
  thyme and rosemary.

- Add some additional fruit,
  like rhubarb, plums or
  cherries.

I'm pretty sure most keen bakers will have an apple pie recipe within their repertoire, whether it's a family classic or a personal favourite. This version, however, offers a bit of a twist, as the caramelized apples sit on top of a creamy layer of frangipane, which adds extra flavour and texture.

I like to use a mixture of apples to maximize flavour: my go-to varieties are Cox's Orange Pippin, Pink Lady, Braeburn and Bramley. That said, using only one variety will still give you a delicious apple pie. This filling is open to many variations: you can change the spices to suit you, vary the additional fruit (though keep the total weight of the fruit the same) or leave it out altogether. Do try the frangipane layer, though: I think it's an apple-pie game-changer.

Line your baking tins with one batch of the pastry and blind-bake and trim according to the instructions on page 13. Leave the baked pastry cases in the tins for filling and finishing.

To make the apple filling, place the sugar, cinnamon, salt and butter in a large saucepan over a low heat and heat gently until everything melts. Tip in the chopped apples and give everything a good stir. Simmer the apples slowly for approximately 15 minutes; the time may vary depending on the varieties used. You want the apple chunks to be softened but still holding their shape rather than collapsing. Strain the apples in a colander, collecting all of the juice in a bowl underneath. Return the juice to the pan and reduce over a medium heat until thick and syrupy – it should look like caramel. The apple flavour in that syrup will become concentrated as it reduces, which will help to ramp up the flavour within the finished pie. Once thickened, take off the heat and stir the apple chunks back in. Set aside to cool, then gently fold through the berries.

To make the frangipane, place the butter and caster sugar in a bowl or stand mixer and beat to combine. Add a third of the ground almonds and mix, then add a splash of the beaten egg and combine. Continue in this manner until all the ground almonds and egg have been added and everything is well combined. Transfer to the fridge until stiffened.

Spread the frangipane over the bottom of the pre-baked pastry cases, then top with the sticky apple mixture and level off neatly. Top with your decorative pastry lids of choice and bake, according to the instructions on page 17.

Geometric Pattern

I have a huge array of cutters and usually have three different sizes for each shape, which allows me to create interesting gradient designs. Here, I used squares and rectangles, gluing each piece in place with egg wash. I cut the small strips using the spaghetti roller on a pasta machine, and I used the tip of a wooden skewer to indent the larger squares.

Basket

This design was a pleasant accident. Although it looks like a basket, it wasn't actually inspired by a basket. Instead, the design evolved through faffing! I started with no real plan, my pastry laid out before me, my pasta machine on hand, as always. After passing long lengths of pastry through the spaghetti cutter, I set about creating. This was the result, and 'the basket' is now one of my signature looks.

This design requires lots of long, thin strips of pastry. To do this, I use my pasta machine. First, roll out the pastry by hand, then cut it into wide strips. Pass these through the plain roller first, set to the widest setting, then pass them through the spaghetti cutter. The longer the strips, the fewer joins will be needed. Mark the working area on your pastry platform as described on page 14, then find the centre point within that area. Using egg wash to act as a glue, brush a small area in the centre. Take one pastry strip and curl the end into a tight spiral. Lay this upon the centre point, then coil the strip around. Continue with the other strips until the outermost edge of the marked area has been reached. Using a ruler and the back of a knife, score marks across the spiral, dividing it into an increasing number of fractions. To finish, decorate with shaped pieces of pastry, adding detail to these with the back of a knife.

ARCHITECTURE

There is so much art in the every day that most of the time we will walk past it unnoticed. Countless expressions in everything from ground level to the very top of the highest buildings. I used to walk with my eyes focused ahead, and even then, looking more at the pavement than around me, my mind focused solely on the destination. Perhaps it was youth, then being a mum so young, a hectic life that blinkered me from the bigger picture. Or perhaps it was because I hadn't yet tapped into my own artistic flair, unable to appreciate or even see the art of others.

Finding my artistic outlet in pastry really did ignite my love of all art. It opened my eyes to how fascinating we can be when we have the courage to express ourselves fully. I could suddenly see art in everything, walking with head lifted, eyes wide, noticing side streets, looking up at buildings. It is amazing what comes into view, things you may have walked past hundreds of times before. Patterned brickwork, inlay, carvings, decorative covings, elaborate skylines created by the most eclectic rooftops. Endless sources of inspiration, and all in everyday scenes, never mind in the intentionally elaborate.

I enjoy visiting churches, cathedrals and places of worship, although I'm not a religious person. I wasn't brought up to be; it's not that I am opposed to being so. However, I am a spiritual person. I am very emotive and perceptive to other's emotions and I'd say I'm also very intuitive. Walking into a cathedral can move me to tears, completely awestruck by the ideas, creativity and visions required to build such a beautiful space. There is inspiration in every nook, upon each door, carved into the stone floors, gilded artworks, stained glass and railings. My eyes are usually drawn to the ceilings, the engineering and vision needed to create them quite simply blow my mind. La Sagrada Familia in Barcelona is something else. I have used such ceilings as design inspiration for my own creations.

Carlisle Cathedral

Above blue, flashed with gold,
an indoor starry sky.

Windows catch the light,
casting colour, bringing life.

Shadows dance, between the aisles,
candles glow with love.

A place of peace, reflection and time,
inspiration high above.

If you can't visit the more architecturally rich towns and cities, do visit your local library. Search for books covering a wide spectrum of architectural design and delve in. It doesn't matter what your preferred style of architecture is, inspiration can be taken from it all. I've personally found some great books over the years in my library, selected at random while walking the aisles.

When re-creating your architecturally inspired designs in pastry, you may find using a pasta machine handy. The perfectly straight and consistent strips that can be cut using both the tagliatelle and spaghetti cutters will be well suited to structured designs.

Lemon Tart

**Makes 1 large tart
or 6 small tarts**

For the pastry

1 batch sweet shortcrust
pastry (page 10)

For the lemon filling

6 eggs

240g (8½oz) caster sugar

zest of 1 lemon

200ml (7fl oz) lemon juice
(about 4 lemons' worth)

175ml (6fl oz) double cream

Variations and additions

• Add vanilla seeds or
  citrus zest to the pastry.

This is a classic crowd-pleaser – I don't think I've ever met anyone who doesn't enjoy a silky slice of perfectly baked lemon tart. This mouth-puckering dessert allows for lots of extra decorative flourishes and artistic flair in the presentation, a great blank canvas to which you can add extra flavour and texture. Express yourself.

Line your baking tin with the pastry and blind-bake and trim according to the instructions on page 13. Leave the baked pastry case in the tin for filling and finishing.

Remove all but one shelf from the oven, and position this remaining shelf near the bottom. Preheat the oven to 140°C/120°C fan/275°F/gas mark 1.

To make the lemon filling, crack the eggs into a large bowl and beat together gently with a fork, taking care not to whisk in too much air. Add the sugar, lemon zest and lemon juice, followed by the cream. Mix together well, then set aside for 10 minutes. You'll notice a reaction between the cream and the lemon juice, which is totally normal – some frothy white bits will appear on the surface. Simply spoon these off and discard, then pass the remaining liquid through a very fine sieve and into a large jug.

Set the tin containing your blind-baked pastry case on a baking sheet and place on the oven shelf, then pour in the lemon mixture. Removing the other oven shelves earlier means you now have space to pour the mixture in easily, right to the very top of the pastry case, without having to move the tart afterwards. Bake for 35 minutes initially; it may need a bit longer, but check at this point. To find out, gently tap the oven shelf with a wooden spoon, and look for movement across the tart's surface. There should be slight ripples towards the centre. If the ripples are reaching towards the edges, leave for 5 more minutes and check again. The tart will set further as it cools, so don't be tempted to bake it until entirely ripple-free! Once you're happy, remove the tart from the oven and leave to cool completely before decorating.

Stained Glass

To make the pastry window, I sketched a simple template, then laid some baking paper over it. I then built up the window frame using strips of hand-cut pastry and used push cutters to add the details. I baked the 'window' separately and topped the tart with it, using an array of small edible flowers and petals to create the technicolour stained-glass effect.

Broderie Anglaise

There is so much inspiration to be found in fabrics and textiles. A wander around a haberdashery or a fabric factory outlet will leave your head bursting with ideas! Broderie Anglaise was the source of inspiration for this design, but you could create a multitude of different patterns using the pastry pieces.

A simple yet effective finish made by pre-baking pastry shapes to lay over the top of the finished tart. Teardrops and circles make up the bulk of the design. The options are endless.

Circles of Fruit

There is no inspiration source here: it's more an expression of feeling, using the fruits, leaves and flowers to create an edible painting. I love the freedom of placement here, and the way the colours work harmoniously with each other. I remember feeling very relaxed when decorating this; even mid-shoot, there was a calm atmosphere, my good friend by my side, the sun blazing. We were happy, grateful for the day and the moment we were sharing. I truly believe those emotions are captured within the finished look of this tart: the most beautiful tart I have created.

A super-sharp knife is needed to cut the fruit this finely. I used a mixture of grapes, plums and apples, along with some blueberries. I made the plum and apple pieces round by cutting them with circular cutters. The leaves used are tagets (marigold): their flavour is citrussy, which complements the tart perfectly.

Nectarine, Peach & Lavender Tart

**Makes 1 large tart
or 6 small tarts**

For the pastry

1 batch sweet shortcrust
pastry (page 10)

**For the lavender crème
pâtissière**

330ml (11fl oz) full-fat milk

1–2 sprigs culinary lavender
(flowerheads only) or 1–2
teaspoons lavender grains

4 egg yolks

80g (2¾oz) caster sugar

35g (1½oz) plain flour

2 teaspoons vanilla bean
paste

For the fruit topping

4–6 nectarines, a mix of
white- and yellow-fleshed
if possible, halved and
stoned

4–6 peaches, a mix of
white- and yellow-fleshed
if possible, halved and
stoned

2 tablespoons smooth
apricot jam

culinary lavender grains,
to finish (optional)

baked pastry shapes
(optional)

This is another tart that really allows for creative freedom in the arrangement of
the fruit pieces. Where I have sliced the nectarines and peaches finely and arranged
randomly in swirls and curls, you could also cut the fruit into chunks – perhaps
eighths or even quarters – and arrange in a more uniform manner. It's really up to
your own mood and interpretation. What I will say is that it is especially important
to use nectarines and peaches that are at their best if you do opt to finely slice
them, as under-ripe fruit will hold little flavour, and the slices won't stand up
to the lavender scented crème on which they are arranged.

Line your tin with the pastry and blind-bake and trim according to the instructions
on page 13. Leave the baked pastry case in the tin for filling and finishing.

Make the crème pâtissière first, as this will need to cool before you assemble the
fruit. In a large saucepan over a medium heat, combine the milk and lavender and
bring to a boil, then take off the heat and leave to infuse for 20 minutes.

Place the egg yolks and two tablespoons of the sugar in a large bowl. Whisk until the
mixture is pale and has some volume. Add the flour and whisk to combine.

Strain the milk to remove the lavender, then return the infused milk to the pan. Add
the remaining sugar and the vanilla and bring to the boil, removing from the heat as
soon as it boils. Pour a little of this hot milk mixture over the egg yolks and mix well,
then add the remainder while whisking continuously. Pour the resulting custard
back into the pan and bring to a gentle boil. Allow the custard to bubble and thicken
for about 2 minutes, whisking all the while. Once it has thickened and the raw flour
has cooked, transfer the custard to a bowl, covering the surface with a layer of
clingfilm before it cools to prevent a skin from forming. Taste for lavender flavour:
if it's enough, great, if you feel a little more is needed, you can add some to the fruit
later. Allow the mixture to cool completely. When you're ready to use, vigorously
whisk the chilled mixture until smooth.

Fill the pre-baked pastry case with the crème pâtissière, saving a little, and level off
neatly. Transfer the remaining crème pâtissière into a piping bag fitted with a small
plain nozzle, or use a piping bag with no nozzle fitted, snipping off the very end.

continued overleaf

Variations and additions

- Add citrus zest to the pastry.

- Use apricots instead of nectarines or peaches.

- Flavour with orange blossom and decorate with French marigold flowers instead of lavender.

Using a sharp knife, slice, cut or chop each of the halved nectarines and peaches and use the fruit to decorate the top of the tart, covering the crème pâtissière completely.

Make a glaze by melting down the apricot jam with a splash of water in a small pan over a low heat until the mixture becomes liquid, but do not let it boil. Use a pastry brush to lightly brush the glaze over the fruit.

This fruit tart will be best assembled and eaten on the day it was made, as the fruit can begin to look a bit tired after that. That said, if stored in the fridge it will keep for up to 3 days, it just won't look as spectacular as when first made.

Graphic Swirls

There is no way to explain how to lay out the fruit for this tart, other than: be free! Don't overthink it. I like to lay out three or four slices in arcs, then rotate the tart tin and lay some more in another direction, continuing until the surface of the crème pâtissière is covered. I also like to flip the fruit slices so they are facing upwards and then tuck them in between so they look like fruit ribbons entwining the design. Pre-baked pastry shapes can be added as an extra, along with piped dots of the saved crème pâtissière. Culinary lavender grains can look pretty sprinkled over the top, but remember they are strong on the palate, so don't overdo it.

Nectarine, Peach & Lavender Pies

**Makes 6 small pies
or 1 large pie**

For the pastry

at least 2 batches sweet
shortcrust pastry (page 10)

For the filling

5 ripe nectarines, halved,
stoned and roughly
chopped, 325g (11½oz)
prepped weight

5 ripe peaches, halved,
stoned and roughly
chopped, 325g (11½oz)
prepped weight

100g (3½oz) caster sugar

pinch of sea salt flakes

80g (2¾oz) unsalted butter

1 teaspoon vanilla bean
paste

½ teaspoon culinary
lavender

2 tablespoons cornflour

Variations and additions

- Try adding either basil,
  thyme or rosemary to the
  fruit mixture. Either as an
  addition or an alternative
  to the lavender.

- Swap some of the
  nectarines or peaches for
  apricots.

I'm not sure there's a more satisfying summer fruit than a perfectly ripe peach.
I remember eating huge peaches in the summers of my childhood, bought by my
nana as a treat when we'd go food shopping in the market hall in town. A peach
would be handed to me in a paper bag, which I'd use to catch the juice as I took those
first few bites. Better than any bag of sweets I ever remember. I relived the memory
of those childhood peaches last year when I saw a selection of huge, perfect peaches
lined up at a friend's deli in London. I tried one; it was the most delicious peach I had
eaten in 40 years.

Those huge, super-ripe peaches seem difficult to source these days; if you're
lucky enough to find them, eat them as they are, straight from the stone. If you're
dealing with supermarket mass-produced, prematurely picked punnets of peaches,
then I suggest you make a pie. You can remove the skins from the fruit if you like;
however, I think it's an unnecessary faff.

Line six individual baking tins with one batch of the pastry and blind-bake and
trim according to the instructions on page 13. Leave the baked pastry cases in
the tins for filling and finishing.

In a saucepan, combine the nectarines, peaches, caster sugar, salt, butter, vanilla
and lavender. Heat over a low heat until the butter melts and the natural juice helps
to dissolve the sugar, then allow to gently simmer for 5–10 minutes (depending on
ripeness). Strain the fruit in a colander, collecting any juice in a bowl below. Return
the juice to the pan and allow to bubble and reduce down until thick and syrupy.
When this is done, take off the heat, then mix with the fruit in a bowl and allow to
cool fully. Taste the fruit at this stage; if you feel it can take a little more lavender,
sprinkle in a few more grains. Do be careful, lavender can be overpowering, which
is why I've suggested starting with quite a small amount. Sprinkle over the cornflour
and stir through.

Fill the pre-baked pastry cases with the cooled fruit mixture and level off neatly.
Top with your decorative pastry lids of choice and bake, according to the
instructions on page 17.

Peruvian Earrings

When searching for new and fresh inspiration, my local library is one of my first ports of call. I feel inspired simply by being surrounded by books, a little part of each author's soul there upon the shelves. This particular design was inspired by a photograph I found in a book about historic cultural fashion: a striking picture of a Peruvian lady with two huge hooped and spiralled earrings in each ear, and an elaborate black headband tied above them.

These tight spirals are made using thin strips of pastry, cut using the spaghetti cutter on a pasta machine. Roll out the pastry by hand first, then pass it through the plain roller of the pasta machine, and then through the spaghetti cutter. Long strips are best, allowing you to make one full spiral without any joins. I used both ends of a piping nozzle to cut out the small and medium circles, then used biscuit cutters for the fluted pieces (see page 206).

Wisteria

Beautiful wisteria: the perfect cascade of purple or white. The sight of a blooming wisteria in early summer will stop me in my tracks; I stand there, soaking up the beauty. I thoroughly enjoyed recreating the trailing flowers.

It looks like there's a lot going on here, however I've actually just used simple push cutters to build up this realistic wisteria flower design. There's no need to glue the pieces in place, which means you can move them if not entirely happy. The leaves were made using a large daisy cutter, the petals cut and used separately, scored with the back of a knife to create the spine detail. Small daisy cutters were used for the flower buds, again using the petals individually. Heart cutters make up the flowers, small balls too, made by rolling up scraps of pastry by hand. The spaghetti cutter on a pasta machine was used for the thin strips. I didn't use a template; I just tried to copy photographs of wisteria I found online.

Dahlias

I have a definite love affair with dahlias, first falling in love with them after admiring the huge and varied blooms that would swamp my Instagram feed during the summer months. These photos went on to fuel a passion for flowers in general, but it's dahlias that have my heart. I am not green-fingered at all, but I do want to grow them and have every intention of growing all the varieties possible at my new home. Until then, there will be dahlia-inspired pies.

These flower pies are created using three different-sized cutters of the same shape, whether that be a circle to make the pompom dahlia or tear-shaped cutters to make the Café au Lait dahlia. Starting at the outer edge of the working area, position your cut-out shapes, making your way around the edge and working towards the centre, using the smaller shapes as you move towards the middle. Add extra 'petals' in places that you feel can be bulked out and mark them with the back of a knife to make them more life-like. Twist some of the petals to create a feeling of movement. Make a centrepiece using small pieces of hand-rolled pastry.

Roasted Spiced Plum & Thyme Pie

**Makes 1 large pie
or 6 small pies**

For the pastry

at least 2 batches sweet
shortcrust pastry (page 10)

For the filling

1kg (2lb 4oz) ripe Victoria
plums, halved and stoned

200g (7oz) light soft brown
sugar, plus extra if needed

80g (2¾oz) unsalted butter,
softened

1 teaspoon ground allspice

1 teaspoon ground
cinnamon

pinch of sea salt flakes

splash of plum or other fruit
liqueur (optional)

a few fresh thyme sprigs,
leaves picked

Variations and additions

- Add vanilla seeds or
  orange zest to the pastry.

- Swap the spices for
  ground cloves, nutmeg
  or star anise.

- Add blackberries, cherries
  or chopped apples

- Experiment with different
  plum varieties.

I had a most bountiful old and gnarly Victoria plum tree in the garden of a house I once lived in, and the fruit it produced every year was incredible. My beloved stepdad Ged would look forward to its yield each year, washing out his old jam pan in anticipation, ready to make that plum jam we all grew to love, and now miss. I would make pies (of course) and the rest of the fruit would be given away to neighbours, or popped in a bucket with a 'help yourself' sign attached. The tree perished in a storm one year, which meant no more plum jam, but the recipe for the pie filling remains.

Roasting the plums is key: it amplifies their flavour and ensures their juice is concentrated. The less excess moisture there is in a pie filling, the better, as it won't spoil the crispness of the pastry, and it also prevents excess steam from being created during baking, which could push your carefully decorated pastry lid out of place.

Line your tin with one batch of the pastry and blind-bake and trim according to the instructions on page 13. Leave the baked pastry case in the tin for filling and finishing.

Preheat the oven to 180°C/160°C fan/350°F/gas mark 4.

Place the halved plums, cut-side up, into a baking dish that will fit them snugly. Sprinkle over the sugar, then add a knob of butter to the top of each plum. Sprinkle over the spices and salt, then drizzle over the liqueur, if using. Finally, scatter with the thyme leaves and place in the oven, uncovered. Roast for 20–30 minutes until the plums are softened and starting to collapse, and their juice is beginning to run. Leave to cool fully, then roughly chop. Add to a bowl, along with any sticky juice that remains in the roasting dish.

Fill the pre-baked pastry case with the cooled fruit, levelling off with a palette knife or similar. Top with your decorative pastry lid of choice and bake, according to the instructions on page 17.

Railings

This fairly elaborate design is made up of very simple shapes. I used small square, circle and daisy push cutters with strips of pastry cut using the tagliatelle cutter on the pasta machine. The design started off quite simple, and I just kept going until I was satisfied. The circular cut-outs were made using the two ends of a piping nozzle.

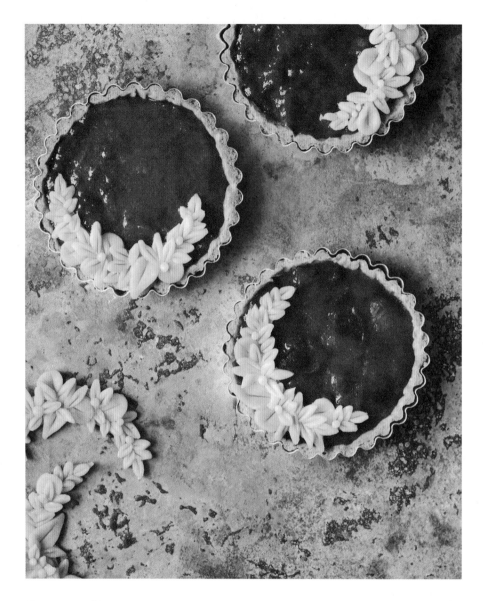

Crescent of Leaves

These crescents were made separately on pieces of baking paper. First, I made a crescent from rolled pastry by cutting out a large circle, then taking most of the circle away using the same cutter. I used a selection of round and tear-shaped cutters, and also a large daisy cutter, from which I cut the individual petals. Try not to overthink the placement: just go for it, alternating the direction and shapes. Adding little balls of pastry is always a favourite finish of mine. Use the back of a knife to add extra detail to the pastry leaves.

Antique Tiles

A friend of mine has the most wonderful kitchen showroom in Carlisle: Carvetii Interiors. The kitchens on display are the stuff of dreams, ranging from the super-slick, light and airy, to dark green and atmospheric. I visit the showroom often, either to work or simply to soak up inspiration. I have made a few pie tops following my visits there. One was inspired by a spectacular wooden door whose texture and design grabbed my interest. The idea for this one came from the patterns painted on some wall tiles on display there.

A little maths and some careful cutting is required here to ensure the 16 squares fit equally within the square pie lid. So calculate the size of the tiles you'll need. First roll the pastry by hand, then pass wide strips through the plain roller of a pasta machine, set to the widest setting. Accurately hand-cut the squares using a ruler and a pizza wheel. The pointed corner pieces were made using a daisy push cutter, cut into four. Pastry balls finish the look.

Plum Rose Tart with Edible Flowers & Crème Pâtissière

**Makes 1 large tart
or 6 small tarts**

For the pastry

1 batch sweet shortcrust
pastry (page 10)

For the crème pâtissière

4 egg yolks

80g (2¾oz) caster sugar

35g (1½oz) plain flour

330ml (11fl oz) full-fat milk

2 teaspoons vanilla bean
paste

For the fruit topping

up to 1kg (2lb 4oz) mixed
plums/gages of your choice,
halved and stoned

2 tablespoons redcurrant
jelly, to glaze (optional)

fresh herbs, edible flowers
and leaves (optional)

Variations and additions

- Add cinnamon, ginger
  or allspice to the crème
  pâtissière.

- Swap the redcurrant jelly
  for apricot or plum.

- Add blackberries, cherries
  or grapes.

- Experiment with different
  plum varieties.

Do try to source a variety of plums for this tart: not only will this provide an array of flavour notes, but the varying skin and flesh colours will look stunning when the fruit is sliced and rolled into plum roses. I always feel like I've hit the jackpot when I find red-fleshed plums and greengages, as they really do add the wow factor, their deep contrasting colours and flavours working beautifully together. If you can't source a selection of plums, one type will work, too. The important thing is that the plums are juicy, tasty and sweet, so do taste them before using.

Make the crème pâtissière first, as this will need to cool before assembling. Place the egg yolks and two tablespoons of the sugar in a large bowl and whisk until the mixture is pale and has some volume. Add the flour and whisk to combine.

In a large saucepan over a medium heat, bring the milk, vanilla and remaining sugar to the boil, removing from the heat as soon as it boils. Pour a little of this hot milk mixture over the egg yolks and mix well, then add the remainder while whisking continuously. Pour the resulting custard back into the pan and bring to a gentle boil. Allow the custard to bubble and thicken for about 2 minutes, whisking all the while. Once it has thickened and the raw flour has been cooked, transfer the custard to a bowl, covering the surface with a layer of clingfilm before it cools to prevent a skin from forming. Allow to cool completely. When ready to use, vigorously whisk until smooth.

Fill the pre-baked pastry case with the crème pâtissière, saving a little, and level off neatly. Transfer the remaining crème pâtissière into a piping bag fitted with a small plain nozzle, or use a piping bag with no nozzle fitted, snipping off the very end.

continued overleaf

Using a super-sharp knife, slice each plum half horizontally into thin slices of around 2mm ($\frac{1}{16}$in). Try to be consistent with your slicing as this will make for a neater plum rose. Lay out between 5 and 8 slices on a clean tea towel, with the rounded sides facing away from you. Each slice should be overlapping the previous one by half. Starting with the first slice laid, roll up (use both hands, it's easier) and keep rolling until the ends of the slices meet. Place in the crème pâtissière, rounded side up: the cream will hold the fruit rose in place. Tweak out the slices a little until it resembles a blooming flower. Repeat until the tart is covered with plum roses.

If you want to glaze the tart, gently melt the redcurrant jelly in a pan over a low heat, along with a splash of water. Don't allow the jelly to boil, as it won't brush easily. Once it's melted, use a delicate brush to brush it over the plum roses, I find using an artist's brush is best for the job. Finish by filling any gaps with cut fruit (green gages work well) and by piping on little dots of crème pâtissière to create lovely contrasting highlights. Finish with any selected herbs, edible leaves and flowers. Beautiful!

This tart is best eaten on the day of assembling, simply because the fruit may begin to look a little tired after that. It will nonetheless keep in the fridge for up to 3 days.

Plum Roses & Leaves *(previous page)*

Randomly place the plum roses across the surface of the tart; I feel the less uniform the placement, the better. Instructions or how to prepare the roses are given within the method. Fill in the gaps with cut fruit and use little dots of crème pâtissière. Place edible flowers, herbs and leaves gently over the top.

Jewellery Cuff *(opposite)*

This was inspired by a Maison Veyret cuff bracelet I found during a late-night Instagram scroll. The design is so aesthetically pleasing and original, and I hugely enjoyed the process of bringing this design to life via pastry.

This design is made up of strips cut using the tagliatelle cutter on a pasta machine and, for the most part, tear-shaped cutters. I started at the bottom, building up the design as I went along, positioning the pieces symmetrically. The small circles were cut using the small end of a piping nozzle, and the hand-rolled balls are consistent in size as I made each one using either half or quarter of a cut circle of pastry. I used edible glitter for a shimmer.

JEWELLERY

I first started using jewellery as inspiration for pie designs after noticing a decorative gold brooch in the window of an antiques shop in Carlisle. I'd never really considered jewellery design to be pie relatable before then, yet the intricate designs and countless formations of jewellery provide an endless source of ideas.

Like everything, the fashions have evolved and changed within jewellery design, and so I found myself delving back through the centuries, finding the Victorian period particularly appealing. Apart from the gems used, the complex metalwork is very pretty indeed. I have a new appreciation for jewellery, it's just a shame my box is empty and I can only admire through windows and books! There are a few designs in this book that were inspired by tribal pieces and stunning ancient Greek, Roman and Egyptian designs. Using these designs opened up a new angle for adding sugar sprinkles and edible glitter to the pastry, which surprisingly hold up during baking.

Looking at jewellery most likely won't result in a direct copy of a ring or necklace on your pie tops, instead be led by the formation of stones perhaps or the way the metal used is shaped. The pie design on page 167 was based on an art deco diamond ring, while the one on page 114 was inspired by a pair of earrings, the elongated shape being the main focus, which I played around with until something unique appeared. I think jewellery-inspired designs have huge scope for experimentation and interpretation. Get that glitter out!

Rhubarb & Apple Tart

**Makes 1 large tart
or 6 small tarts**

For the pastry

1 batch sweet shortcrust
pastry (page 10)

For the frangipane

80g (2¾oz) unsalted butter,
at room temperature

80g (2¾oz) caster sugar

80g (2¾oz) ground almonds

80g (2¾oz) beaten egg

For the syrup

100g (3½oz) caster sugar,
plus extra for dusting

50ml (1¾oz) water

2 star anise (optional)

1 teaspoon vanilla bean
paste

pinch of sea salt flakes

For the fruit topping

juice of 2 lemons

3 eating apples

4–8 rhubarb stems,
depending on thickness,
chopped into 2cm (¾in)
pieces

Rhubarb is great for creating show-stopping tarts. Using the interior of the rhubarb stems to create a two-toned finish gives limitless options for creating graphic or intricate designs, so let your imagination – and patience level! – guide you. Do try to source rhubarb stems that are as equal in thickness as possible, as you will find your rhubarb tiles will slot together much more easily, allowing stunning patterns to emerge before your eyes.

My favourite time of year to make these tarts is when the bright blush- and crimson-coloured stems of forced rhubarb are available. They create the most incredible candy-striped kaleidoscope of pinks and whites. That said, the green stems I used to make the tart opposite are beautiful too. Admittedly, these tarts have more wow factor pre-bake, but with careful baking under foil, you will achieve a beautiful, almost antiqued, finish post-bake.

Line your tin with the pastry and blind-bake and trim according to the instructions on page 13. Leave the baked pastry case in the tin for filling and finishing. Any excess pastry can be used for decoration.

To make the frangipane, place the butter and caster sugar in a bowl or stand mixer and beat to combine. Try not to incorporate too much air, as you don't want the frangipane to puff up too much during baking, or it might displace the carefully arranged rhubarb. Add a third of the ground almonds and mix, then add a splash of the beaten egg and combine. Continue in this manner until all the ground almonds and egg have been added and everything is well combined. Transfer to the fridge to stiffen.

Meanwhile, make a flavoured sugar syrup. Simply combine the sugar, water, star anise (if using), vanilla and salt in a small saucepan and set over a medium heat until the sugar dissolves and the liquid reduces to a syrupy consistency. Remove from the heat.

Once the frangipane is cool, spread it across the base of the pre-baked pastry case, levelling it out neatly.

continued overleaf

Variations and additions

- Skip the apple swirls and just use rhubarb (if you do this, you will need more rhubarb stems).

- Make the frangipane with cooled browned butter (see page 99).

- Swap the ground almonds for ground pistachios or ground macadamia nuts.

- Flavour the syrup with different spices, such as ginger, cardamom, cinnamon or nutmeg

To prepare the apples, heat a large pan of water until simmering and add the juice of 1 lemon. Prepare a bowl of cold water (with ice if possible), and add the juice of the remaining lemon to this. Core the apples with an apple corer, then halve each vertically. Slice each half horizontally, as thinly as possible, then plunge the apple slices into the simmering water and allow them to soften until pliable. Keep checking them every 30 seconds or so. When they're ready, the slices should be able to bend and curl without breaking. Drain, then plunge the slices into the cold water to stop them from softening further.

Lay the rhubarb pieces on top of the frangipane in a decorative fashion – you may want to use different sized pieces, and if you want to expose the interior colour of the rhubarb, simply trim off the skin from the flat side of the stems. Use the prepared apple slices to either make decorative swirls, pushing them into the frangipane to hold their shape, or make apple roses following the method on page 29. If you're using decorative pastry shapes, add these too.

When you're done, brush the surface of the fruit with the flavoured syrup using a pastry brush, avoiding any pastry shapes used. If the syrup has solidified, simply warm through until it becomes liquid enough to use. Any pastry shapes can be egg-washed, but this isn't completely necessary. Place the tart in the fridge for at least 1 hour or even overnight to chill before baking.

Place a baking sheet in the oven and preheat to 160°C/140°C fan/325°F/gas mark 3.

Sprinkle the entire surface of the tart with a fine dusting of caster sugar before covering it loosely with foil. The tart can take up to 2 hours to bake: the time will vary depending on how the fruit is laid and sliced, and, of course, your oven. I suggest checking after the first hour, then every 20 minutes thereafter, removing the foil for the final 20 minutes of baking. The tart is ready when the fruit has softened and you can see that the frangipane has a sponge-like appearance.

Remove from the oven and allow to cool before removing from the tin.

Jewellery Box *(page 67)*

Vintage jewellery boxes were as carefully crafted as the jewels they once held; each box designed to hold the gems within perfectly. With leather exteriors and soft velvet or silk cushions inside, I find these lovely boxes inspirational in their own right.

Using the contrasting colours of the interior and exterior of the rhubarb can create countless patterns. Work with what you have – perhaps leave some stems intact but halved vertically, and chop others evenly before arranging on the frangipane. For the apple swirls, follow the instructions within the recipe and place in a carefree manner until you are happy. Plaited pastry makes the border and tear-shaped cutters can be used to add leaves.

Parquet

This parquet design requires accurate cutting of pastry tiles: to fit together perfectly, they need to be cut to 1 x 3cm (½ x 1¼in). I suggest using a pasta roller to give you consistent and perfectly rolled pastry. Roll out the pastry by hand first, then cut it into wide strips and pass through the plain roller of the pasta machine, set to the widest setting. Then use a ruler and a small, sharp kitchen knife to mark out the measurements. Use a pizza wheel and the ruler to cut the pastry into tiles. Have a pastry platform ready, marked out with a working area (see page 14). Lay the ruler across the middle of the marked area and very gently score a line in the pastry and use this line as a starting point. Using egg wash and an artist's brush, gently coat small areas at a time and start laying the tiles in a 3 by 3 format, alternating between vertical and horizontal placement. The egg wash will glue the tiles in place. Continue until the working area is covered, going slightly over the edges of the marked-out circle; you can trim off the excess later.

Six Lattices

All of the strips used for the six different lattices shown here were cut using the tagliatelle cutter on a pasta machine. Roll the pastry by hand, then cut into wide strips to pass through the plain roller of the pasta machine on the widest setting. Next, pass the strips through the tagliatelle cutter. For each lattice design, start by laying strips side by side vertically, across a pastry platform marked with your working area (see page 14). Starting on the left-hand side, lift either one, two or three strips, leaving the next one, two or three in place, and so on. Lay one, two or three strips horizontally, then replace the lifted vertical strips back over them. Continue like this, but lift and replace alternating sets of strips each time, creating a weave effect.

Butterfly

*Life's challenges can force us to make changes: we have to adapt, reinvent, refresh and
sometimes start completely anew. I had to do just that after my divorce. I was suddenly on
my own, with two young children to care for, numerous plates to keep spinning, and no one
there to help. The reality of my new situation was undoubtedly daunting, but on the flip side,
it was my second chance, and the excitement at starting a new life was liberating. This butterfly
is a representation of me starting over; it signifies change and transition from old to new.*

Print out a butterfly shape and use it to cut out the shape from rolled-out pastry. Lay this
on top of a pastry platform (see page 14), then use extra pastry and all kinds of different-
shaped cutters to build up an intricate and elaborate design.

Rhubarb Pie

**Makes 1 large pie
or 6 small pies**

For the pastry

at least 2 batches sweet
shortcrust pastry (page 10)

For the filling

800g (1lb 12oz) trimmed
rhubarb, cut into 2cm (¾in)
chunks

2 tablespoons water

200g (7oz) caster sugar

80g (2¾oz) unsalted butter

1 teaspoon vanilla bean
paste

2 star anise (optional)

pinch of sea salt flakes

1 eating apple, peeled, cored
and finely chopped (about
160g/5¾oz)

125g (4½oz) fresh
raspberries

Variations and additions

- Add vanilla seeds or lemon
  zest to the pastry.

- Use different spices, such
  as cinnamon, cardamom,
  ginger or nutmeg.

- Swap the raspberries for
  blackberries, blueberries
  or strawberries, or leave
  out the berries and apple
  altogether and have
  a rhubarb-only filling
  (ensure the total fruit
  weight remains the same).

Rhubarb is so distinct and unique, there really is no comparison. I absolutely adore the flavour: sharp, sour and unquestionable. This is my favourite way to enjoy rhubarb: rounded off perfectly with sugar, gently simmered with a splash of water and some star anise, then paired with some extra fruit. There's just something about this combination of flavours.

For maximum flavour it is important to reduce the cooking juice from the rhubarb before you return it to the finished filling. If you end up with more filling than required, you can use it by spooning it over something creamy, like warm rice pudding, thick Greek yogurt or a silky panna cotta.

Line your tin with one batch of the pastry and blind-bake and trim according to the instructions on page 13. Leave the baked pastry case in the tin for filling and finishing.

In a large saucepan, combine the rhubarb, water, sugar, butter, vanilla, star anise (if using) and salt. Set over a medium heat and allow to gently cook until the rhubarb has softened but isn't collapsing. This doesn't take long: it could be anywhere between 5 and 10 minutes depending on the rhubarb, so do be careful, keep a close eye on it, as you don't want it to turn to mush. When the rhubarb is soft but still holding its shape, drain well, collecting the juice. Set aside the strained fruit in a bowl and return the juice to the pan, still over a medium heat. Allow to bubble until reduced, thickened and syrupy. Be patient with this, it can take up to 15 minutes. When the syrup is thick and sticky and has a strong, concentrated rhubarb flavour, add enough of it to the cooked rhubarb to bind – around 4 tablespoons is usually adequate. Do keep any leftover syrup, though, as it is delicious, especially over ice cream.

Add the chopped apple and raspberries to the rhubarb mixture and gently stir, then set aside to cool completely.

Use the cooled fruit to fill the pre-baked pastry case, levelling off with a palette knife or similar. Top with your decorative pastry lid of choice and bake, according to the instructions on page 17.

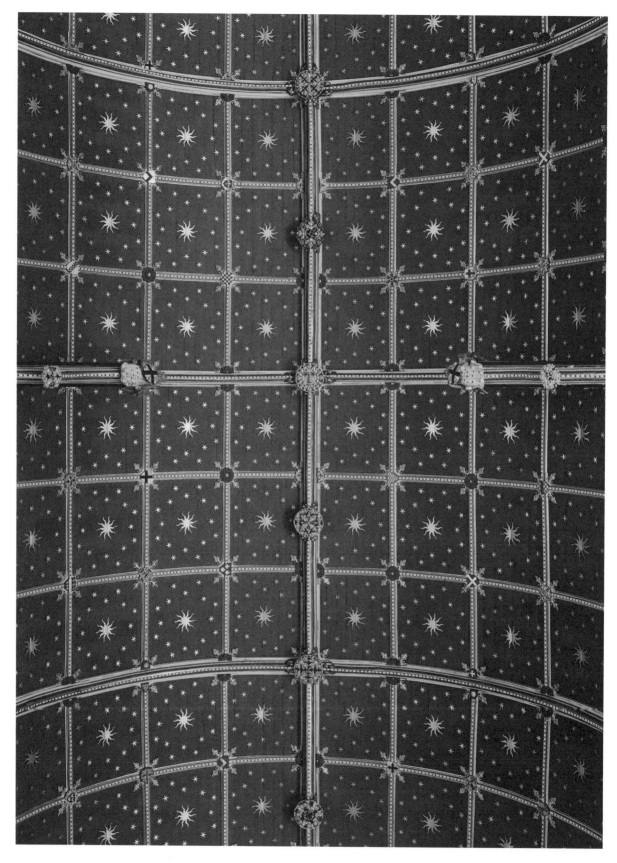

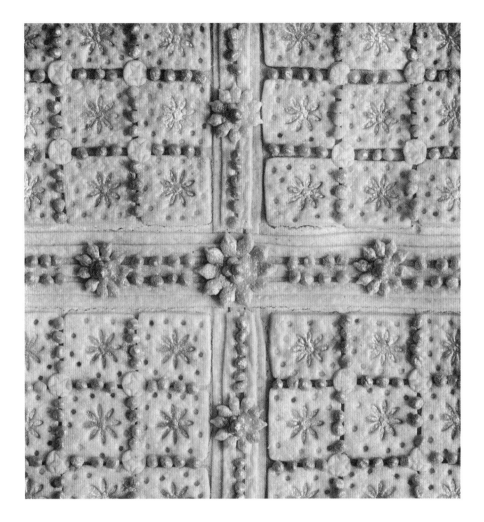

Carlisle Cathedral Ceiling

For a relatively small city, the cathedral in Carlisle is grand. The artistry is stunning, the stained-glass windows huge, and the ceiling is breath-taking and unusual. When you look up, bright blue squares punctuated with gold stars meet your gaze, like a starry sky.

A little maths is required when working out the design for this one to ensure that the squares fit equally within the quarter sections. Mark out the working area on your pastry platform (see page 14) and then calculate as required. Either hand-cut the squares using a ruler and a pizza wheel, or, if you're lucky, you may find you have a square cutter that is the right size. For the central strips, use the tagliatelle cutter on a pasta machine. Then for consistency in the size of the pastry balls, use a small press cutter and roll the pastry in the palm of your hand. Use daisy cutters for the star/flower shapes: pinching the petal points makes them look more antique. A flower stamp and a wooden skewer may be used to indent the pastry tiles, and a gentle brushing of edible gold glitter added to finish.

Dairy

Mamma's Mince & Cheddar Cheese Pies

CHEDDAR

Makes 6 small pies or 1 large pie

For the pastry base

at least 2 batches savoury shortcrust pastry (page 11)

For the filling

2 tablespoons vegetable oil, for frying

1 onion, finely diced, 125g (4½oz) prepped weight

250g (9oz) minced beef

2 large carrots, peeled and finely chopped, 150g (5½oz) prepped weight

1 teaspoon sea salt flakes

2 teaspoons freshly ground black pepper

40g (1½oz) Bisto gravy granules (or your favourite beef gravy granules)

570ml (18fl oz) boiling water

100g (3½oz) best-quality strong-flavoured Cheddar, grated

Variations and additions

- Try adding freshly ground black pepper to the pastry.

- Add chopped parsley or a splash of Worcestershire sauce to the mince mixture.

- Swap the minced beef for soy mince and use vegetable gravy granules for a vegetarian option.

There was nothing fancy about my mum's mince. It was simple food, made quickly with an onion, carrots, shop-bought gravy granules and plenty of pepper, with not a herb in sight – but oh, it was good. She'd serve it with a spoonful of mash, or as a cottage pie, the best comforting Mamma food. Is there anything better? When I discovered a recipe for mince and cheese pies, my mum's mince instantly sprang to mind, so I set about making my own version.

Line six individual tins with one batch of the pastry and blind-bake and trim according to the instructions on page 13. Leave the baked pastry cases in the tins for filling and finishing.

Heat the oil in a large saucepan over a medium heat. Add the onion and fry for a couple of minutes until softened and starting to colour, then add the mince and break it up in the pan with a wooden spoon or spatula. Stir well until the meat changes colour. My mum never bothered with a deep browning of the mince, so let's stay true to her method here and just cook it until it changes from pink to light brown. Add the carrots and salt and pepper, along with the gravy granules and boiling water.

Bring to the boil, then reduce the heat to low and simmer for 30 minutes, by which time the carrots will be tender, and the gravy nice and thick. Check for seasoning: it should be peppery, do add a bit more pepper if it isn't quite coming through strongly enough. Allow to cool completely.

Transfer the mince mixture to the pre-baked pastry cases, then cover with the grated cheese and level off. Top with your decorative pastry lids of choice and bake, according to the instructions on page 17.

These pies are best served warm, but could be cooled and eaten cold.

Abstract Thyme

Roll out the pastry platforms and mark out your working area (see page 14). The thin strips here were cut using the spaghetti cutter on a pasta machine. I made the little leaves using a small oval push cutter. I laid these out carefully, using egg wash to glue the 'leaves' in place.

EMOTIONS

Inspiration needn't come from the physical, in fact the designs that I am most happy with and connected to, come from within. When I post these images, they seem to stand out somehow, they will gain more engagement on social media, even though the viewer can't know that I was driven by emotion at the time of making. Drawing upon personal feelings and experiences when creating is of course how some of the best, memorable and moving songs, books, poems and artworks come to fruition. The finest and most awe-inspiring designs throughout the artistic world are made by those willing to give everything, through the creative process they bear their heart and soul.

I'm not saying that designing in pastry will ever be on the same level as writing a classic song or painting a masterpiece, but the creative process is as rewarding. Tapping into your own creative flair will be soothing and liberating and, once it's ignited, it needn't and shouldn't stop at playing with pastry. When I started making pretty pies, pastry was my then therapy, with all of the designs made with no outside inspiration, everything purely from the heart. Mindful and time-consuming faffing helped me to forget that my mum was forgetting me. Channelling those emotions creatively not only helped me cope, it set me upon a career I never imagined possible. Not only that: with creativity sparkling, I found myself feeling more alive than I had in years. New interests followed – photography, writing, poetry – and I embraced music with renewed vigour. I will do everything I can to learn to play the guitar, as soon as time allows. Who knows, I may even try to write some songs in the future too.

When drawing upon your emotions for inspiration, include experiences good and bad, feel the connection to that moment or what the memory is bringing to you. I find listening to music helps, selecting a genre that will amplify those feelings. Make a start straight away, or think about the relevance of the emotion.

Tree

If you ever have the opportunity to visit Kew Gardens, in southwest London, do go. I visited for the first time in the summer of 2020, when we were allowed to travel again after lockdown. I think the sense of freedom made the visit especially liberating. There is so much to enjoy in Kew, but the one thing that stopped me in my tracks was the most perfect tree I had ever seen. Trees are amazing, and inspiring.

I made the tree trunk and branches using thin strips of pastry cut using the spaghetti cutter on my pasta machine. First, pass hand-rolled pastry through the plain roller, set to the widest setting, then pass that through the spaghetti cutter. Lay this out on a pastry platform, with the working area marked out (see page 14). I made the leaves using a small daisy push cutter, with the individual petals cut off. I pinched the tips to make them more leaf-like and used the back of a knife to indent.

Love

Love is inspiring. Love is everything. Life is grey without it. I've been there. Even though you can be told you are loved, if you don't feel it, it can seem non-existent: empty words that neither comfort nor inspire. When love isn't reciprocated, it hurts; when it is, it is fireworks. Love is magic. Love fuels creativity.

I used the 'L' as my starting point, which I created using strips of pastry, cut using the spaghetti cutter on the pasta machine. I used a tiny daisy push cutter to create the wording, with more spaghetti pastry used to outline the 'o', 'v' and 'e'. I made the rest of the design by framing the word using thicker strips of pastry, which I cut using the tagliatelle cutter. I used tear-shaped cutters for the leaves, creating the indent with the back of a knife.

Spinach & Feta Pie

**Makes 1 large pie or tart
or 6 small pies or tarts**

For the pastry

at least 2 batches savoury
shortcrust pastry (page 11)

For the filling

6 tablespoons olive oil

250g (9oz) baby spinach,
stalks removed

1 large garlic clove, very
finely sliced

100g (3½oz) feta, finely
crumbled

180g (6¼oz) goat's curd

2 eggs

30g (1oz) pine kernels,
toasted

nutmeg, for grating

2 tablespoons finely
chopped flat-leaf parsley
leaves

1 teaspoon dried mint

¼ teaspoon dried chilli
flakes, optional

sea salt flakes and freshly
ground black pepper

Variations and additions

- Add ground nutmeg
  to the pastry.

- Add mustard seeds
  to the filling.

- Stir some raisins into
  the filling mixture for
  extra flavour.

Spinach and feta is a classic combination that doesn't need much playing around with; however, the odd, carefully considered addition can only be a good thing. Here, I've added a tangy hit with the addition of some goat's curd. If you like, you could also add a few raisins to offer a balancing sweetness. It all makes for a delightful vegetarian pie packed full of flavour and goodness. This is perfect for a summer lunch, served al fresco with wine.

Line your tin with one batch of the pastry and blind-bake and trim according to the instructions on page 13. Leave the baked pastry case in the tin for filling and finishing.

Gently heat half of the olive oil in a large saucepan over a low heat. Add the spinach, season with a good pinch of salt and a grinding of pepper, and cook for a couple of minutes, tossing the leaves with some kitchen tongs until fully wilted. Add the garlic and cook for another minute or so, then remove from the pan and leave in a colander to drain off any excess liquid.

Put the feta and goat's curd in a food processor with the remaining olive oil and the eggs. Pulse until combined and smooth, then transfer to a large bowl. Squeeze the spinach to remove any final moisture, then roughly chop. Stir it into the feta mixture until well combined, then add the remaining ingredients. Taste and add a little more salt only if needed.

Fill the pre-baked pastry with the feta and spinach mixture, then top with your decorative pastry lid of choice and bake, according to the instructions on page 17.

I think this pie is as tasty served hot as it is cold. Whichever is your preference, it will always be best eaten on the day it was made. If any remains, it could be stored in the fridge for up to 3 days.

Weave

All of the strips used for lattice shown were cut using the tagliatelle cutter on a pasta machine. The basic technique used to create a weave or lattice effect is explained on page 71. I used a few different weaves on the pie shown, lifting and laying impulsively rather than aiming for a uniform weave. The options are endless. For inspiration, just do an online search for 'basket weaves' – you'll get so many ideas!

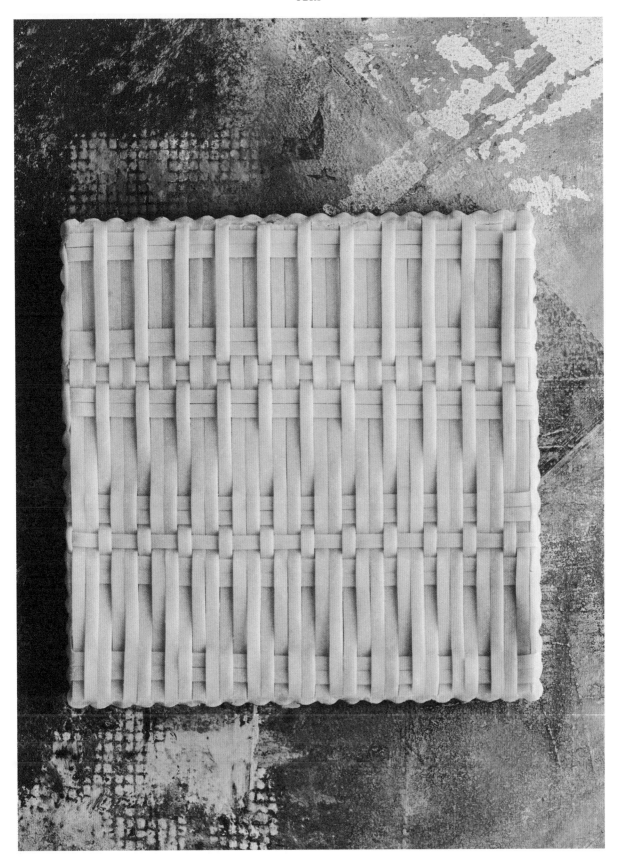

SPINACH & FETA TART

The filling above can also be used to make a delicious tart. Simply line your tin with one batch of savoury shortcrust pastry (page 11) and blind-bake and trim according to the instructions on page 13. Leave the baked pastry case in the tin for filling and finishing. Any excess pastry can be used for decoration.

Preheat the oven to 140°C/120°C fan/275°F/gas mark 1.

Place the tin containing the pre-baked pastry case on a baking sheet and fill the case with the creamy spinach mixture, filling as close to the top of the tin as possible. Bake for 25 minutes, then check. There should be slight movement across the surface. The tart will set further as it cools. If it needs a little longer, bake for another 5 minutes and check again. Allow to cool slightly before removing from the tin. Serve warm or cold, adding separately cooked pastry garnishes if you wish.

Peacock Feathers

The pastry used for the feathers were rolled and cut by passing through the pasta machine. First, pass through the plain roller, set to the widest setting, then through the spaghetti cutter. Search online for peacock feather templates and print out your favourite. Cut out and use as a template to cut feathers from rolled-out pastry. The feathers will be baked separately from the tart, so work on baking paper. Brush with egg wash. Using the spaghetti strips, first create the central spine down the middle of the feathers, then lay strips side by side on either side of the spine to replicate the feather's strands. There's no need to measure the strips: just lay them down, then pull to break at the right point. Add a second layer of strips – not too many this time, just enough to create some 'movement' by placing the strands in slightly different directions. To make the 'eyes' of the feathers, create a spiral using the spaghetti pastry. Chill the feathers well before baking at 200°C/180°C fan/400°F/gas mark 6 until golden – this will take 12–15 minutes.

Cheddar and Onion Pie

**Makes 1 large pie
or 6 small pies**

For the pastry

at least 2 batches savoury
shortcrust pastry (page 11)

For the filling

50g (1¾oz) salted butter

2 onions finely sliced, 300g
(10½oz) prepped weight

1 tablespoon fresh thyme
leaves

200g (7oz) waxy potatoes,
sliced

500ml (18fl oz) vegetable
stock

sea salt flakes and freshly
ground black pepper

For the cheese sauce

50g (1¾oz) salted butter

2 tablespoons plain flour

250ml (9fl oz) milk

160g (5¾oz) strong
farmhouse Cheddar, grated

3 teaspoons mustard

small bunch of flat-leaf
parsley, finely chopped

½ teaspoon freshly ground
black pepper

Variations and additions

• Add mustard powder to the
pastry.

• Fry some caraway seeds
with the onions.

The secret to success with this pie filling is maxing out the flavour of the onions and being bold with the cheese sauce. Use the strongest Cheddar you can find, go heavy with the mustard and take your time when cooking the onions. It makes for a truly delicious pie, perfect served alongside mouth-puckering pickles.

Line your tin with one batch of the pastry and blind-bake and trim according to the instructions on page 13. Leave the baked pastry case in the tin for filling and finishing.

Melt the butter in a large sauté pan over a medium heat, and add the onions, thyme and a good pinch of salt. Reduce the heat to low and slowly cook the onions until soft and just starting to turn golden – this shouldn't be rushed, and can take up to 25 minutes. Stir occasionally to prevent the onions catching on the bottom of the pan.

Add the potatoes, along with a generous grinding of pepper, and stir to combine, then add the stock. Leave to simmer, uncovered, for around 10 minutes or until the potatoes are soft. Drain and allow the potato mixture to cool.

To make the sauce, add the butter and flour to a saucepan over a medium heat. Allow the butter to melt and the flour to sizzle for a minute, then pour in the milk and whisk continuously until the mixture thickens. Allow the sauce to bubble over a low heat for 5 minutes before adding the cheese, then stir in the mustard. Pour over the potato mixture. Stir through the parsley and pepper and allow to cool fully.

Fill the pre-baked pastry case with the potato mixture and level off the surface. Top with your decorative pastry lid of choice and bake, according to the instructions on page 17.

This pie is as delicious hot as it is cold. Whichever is your preference, it will always be best eaten on the day it is made.

Gold Brooch

There is a little curiosity shop beside Carlisle Cathedral that sells all kinds of things. They have a few jewellery cases, and in one of these I spotted a gold brooch with a very beautiful design. My first thought upon seeing it was: 'That will make a great pie top!' Pie inspiration is everywhere!

Mark the working area on your pastry platform as described on page 14, then mark out circles within it and use pastry strips twisted together to lay over the circles. Use different-shaped cutters to build up the design. Here, the small circles were cut out using the small end of a piping nozzle. A daisy cutter was used too, then I cut each flower into three pieces to create the design in the outer circle.

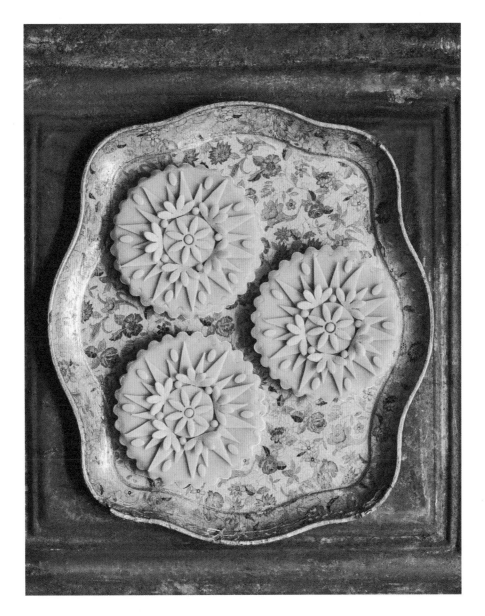

Starburst

I made these patterns using a combination of push cutters and hand-cutting using a printed star template, which I found online.

Lupins *(overleaf)*

The pastry stems and tendrils were made by rolling pastry between my fingers and the work surface. For the leaves, I used a pointed daisy cutter with the petals cut and placed individually. I used different-sized heart cutters to create the lupin flowerheads, placing them along the stem in different directions and in several layers.

The Path

Drifting along, upon a breeze
single white feathers flew.
The circling air, it held my hand
spring flowers in full view.

Sweet violets, primrose, show the way,
of a track I seem to know,
through the woodland, out to fields,
a gentle stream in flow.

Over a gate entwined with leaves,
a hidden path of healing,
leading out to daisied view,
flowers full of meaning.

The weeks pass, I walk the path,
each month bringing new.
Different flowers now in sight,
forget-me-nots, white and blue.

Butterflies now lead the way,
the rambling roses catching.
Along the route now well walked,
foxglove and wild lupin.

The path now, only tangled grass,
the flowers gone to seed.
Bramble bushes bearing fruit,
fields of grains and common reed.

Berry jewelled hedgerows,
leaves, amber in the trees.
Nature and her beauty scenes.
Autumn sun, gentle breeze.

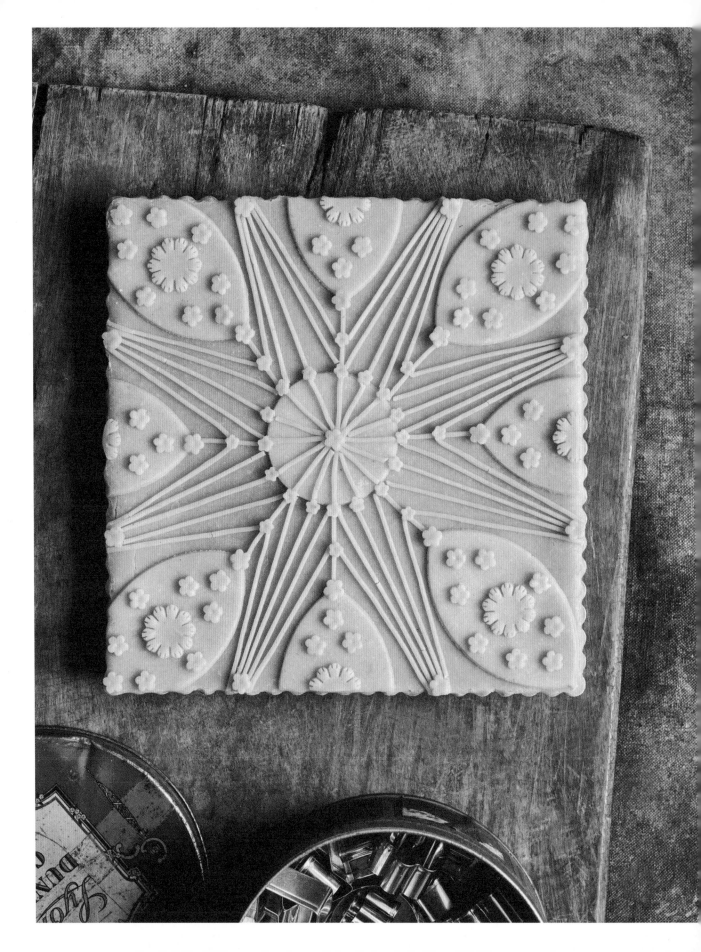

Camembert, Ham & Redcurrant Pie

**Makes 1 large pie
or 6 small pies**

For the pastry

at least 2 batches savoury
shortcrust pastry (page 11)

For the filling

50g (1¾oz) salted butter

2 tablespoons plain flour

200ml (7fl oz) milk

nutmeg, for grating

100g (3½oz) honey-roast
ham, roughly chopped

200g (7oz) Camembert,
cut into 1cm (½in) cubes

50g (1¾oz) fresh or frozen
redcurrants (optional)

3 tablespoons redcurrant
jelly

Variations and additions

- Try adding herbs, such
  as parsley, thyme or
  rosemary, to the ham and
  cheese mixture.

- Stir in some pine kernels
  or roasted garlic for added
  flavour and texture.

- Try swapping the ham
  for a vegetable such
  as roasted peppers or
  onions.

Oozing, hot Camembert is a food of true indulgence, and is one of my all-time favourite things to eat. Admittedly, I usually just bake a whole cheese and enjoy it with crusty bread, but baking it within a pastry case adds a bit of drama and, of course, allows for that artistic finish with the pastry.

Line your tin with one batch of the pastry and blind-bake and trim according to the instructions on page 13. Leave the baked pastry case in the tin for filling and finishing.

Place the butter and flour in a saucepan over a medium heat. Leave the butter to melt and the flour to sizzle for a minute, then pour in the milk, whisking continuously until thickened. Reduce the heat to low and allow the sauce to bubble for 5 minutes, then add the nutmeg to taste and the salt and mix well. Transfer to a bowl to cool completely.

Once cool, stir through the ham, cubed cheese and the redcurrants (if using), ensuring all are evenly coated with the sauce.

Spread the redcurrant jelly over the base of the pre-baked pastry case, then top that with the cheese and ham mixture. Level off the surface with a palette knife. Top with your decorative pastry lid of choice and bake, according to the instructions on page 17.

Serve hot while the cheese is still melting, but do allow the pie to cool for 5 minutes before slicing.

Gaudí Architecture

The design opposite was inspired by the ceiling in La Sagrada Familia in Barcelona. While this is nowhere near as complex (I couldn't even attempt that), it is striking and heavily influenced by the mix of textures, shapes and focal points. Gaudí was a true visionary and very brave in his design.

First, roll out the pastry platform, and mark out the working area with the baking tin being used (see page 14). The shape of an oval baking tin was traced to create the corner shapes then some were halved and used in between. A circular cutter was used for the central piece and the thin strips of pastry were made using the spaghetti cutter of a pasta roller. Small and medium daisy push cutters along with a carnation cutter were used to create the floral part of the design.

Feathers

A pasta roller is used to create the feathers. First, pass pastry through the plain roller, set to the widest setting, then through the spaghetti cutter. Search for a feather shape online and print out your favourite, then cut it out to use as a template. Cut feathers from rolled-out pastry, then lay them on a pastry platform with your working area marked out (see page 14). Brush with egg wash, then use the spaghetti strips to create a central spine down the middle of the feathers. Next, lay strips side by side on either side of the spine to replicate the feathers' strands. There's no need to measure the strips; just lay them down, then pull to break at the right point. Add a second layer of strips, but don't use too many this time: just enough to create some 'movement' by placing the strands in slightly different directions. Use edible glitter and sprinkles to finish.

Goat's Cheese, Roasted Pumpkin & Garlic Pie

**Makes 1 large pie
or 6 small pies**

For the pastry

at least 2 batches savoury
shortcrust pastry (page 11)

For the filling

100ml (3½fl oz) light olive oil

1 whole garlic bulb, skin on,
with the very top sliced off

820g (1lb 13oz) Delicia, Kent
or Kabocha pumpkin, or
butternut squash, deseeded
but skin left on, chopped
into large chunks

4 large banana shallots,
halved lengthways, skin on

1 teaspoon fennel seeds

small bunch of fresh thyme

100g (3½oz) salted butter

nutmeg, for grating
(optional)

150g (5½oz) goat's cheese,
such as Ragstone, sliced
into 0.5cm (¼in) slices

sea salt flakes and freshly
ground black pepper

I'm a huge fan of goat's cheese, especially when partnered with something sweet yet savoury. Here, that element is provided by roasted pumpkin (or squash) along with some softened garlic. Roasting rather than boiling the pumpkin is key: the flavour will be intensified during the process, and the pumpkin will lose some of its excess moisture, helping to keep the pastry crisp.

My favourite soft goat's cheese is Ragstone, but you can use your own favourite; even a blue variety would work. Some types can go grainy when overheated, but the encasing pumpkin will protect the cheese, keeping the texture just right.

Line your tin with one batch of the pastry and blind-bake and trim according to the instructions on page 13. Leave the baked pastry case in the tin for filling and finishing.

Preheat the oven to 200°C/180°C fan/400°F/gas mark 6.

Drizzle a little of the olive oil over the top of the garlic bulb where the cloves are exposed, then wrap the whole thing in foil. Place the chunks of pumpkin or squash in a deep roasting tray with the shallots, fennel seeds and thyme, and drizzle with the remaining oil. Mix well. Sprinkle with salt and pepper and place the wrapped garlic in the tray too. Roast for 50 minutes, then cover the tray with foil and roast for about another 20 minutes. The pumpkin flesh should be super tender, the shallots should be charred yet sweet, and the garlic cloves should be soft enough to squeeze from their skins. When ready, remove the tray from the oven and set aside to cool.

Meanwhile, brown the butter in a small saucepan over a medium heat, making sure it doesn't burn. This takes around 5 minutes. When done, pass through a metal sieve, then allow the strained butter to cool but not solidify. Set aside.

Once the roasted vegetables are cool, remove and discard the skin from the pumpkin, shallots and garlic, being careful to discard any overly charred bits. Add half of each to a food processor, along with the browned butter, then blitz to a super-smooth purée. Grate in nutmeg to taste, if using. Taste the mixture and add some salt if needed.

Roughly chop the remaining vegetables and place them in a bowl, then add the purée and stir to combine.

continued overleaf

Variations and additions

- Omit the fennel and nutmeg and use your favourite spices instead.

- Add some fresh parsley to the mixture before baking.

- Swap the goat's cheese for Brie or Camembert.

Spread half the pumpkin mixture across the base of the pre-baked pastry case, then top that with as many slices of the goat's cheese as possible, filling in any gaps with cut-up pieces. Cover with the remaining pumpkin mixture, then flatten out the surface. Top with your decorative pastry lid of choice and bake, according to the instructions on page 17.

Allow to cool for 5 minutes before slicing. My preference is to eat this pie warm, but it is delicious cold too.

Pasta Pastry

My second favourite way to use flour is to make fresh pasta. I can sit and shape pasta dough for hours. I rarely watch TV, but when I do it's usually with a few trays set out before me, pasta dough rolled and cut, my hands rhythmically folding it into shapes. The design on the previous page was inspired by those hours of pasta-shaping, and as I use my pasta machine more often for pastry than I do for pasta, the two hobbies were bound to collide at some point.

This is a dramatic and effective look that requires more patience than skill. First, roll out the pastry platform and mark out the working area (see page 14). To make the shapes even and consistent, pass the pastry through the plain roller of the pasta machine, set to its widest setting. Then, use a small round cutter to make circles, before nipping two sides of each circle together. Use an egg wash on the pastry platform in sections, to glue and hold the shapes in place.

Triangle Lattice

This lattice is woven on the diagonal; it's surprising how the direction of the weave can change the look so much. First, roll out the pastry platform and mark out the working area (see page 14), then roll more pastry and pass it through the plain roller of a pasta machine, set to the widest setting. Next, use the width of a ruler to cut the pastry into even strips. To weave, lay these strips side by side, then lay the ruler diagonally across the middle of the strips. Lift alternate strips, resting them gently across the ruler, then lay another strip of pastry across the unlifted ones. Return the lifted strips and repeat the process until you reach the bottom of the marked area, before repeating for the top half. To create the triangle effect, run a pasta wheel through the cross points of the lattice. Add pastry balls at the cross sections, and pastry leaves made using a push cutter across the middle.

Pressed Glass

This really is a super-fast, easy and effective finish, perfect for when time is tight but the 'wow' factor is still desired. Simply press the pastry lids against cut class plates to emboss the pastry with the plates' design. Edible glitter can be brushed on to finish the look. Do take time to press the pattern firmly into the pastry, so that none of the pattern is lost during baking.

Taleggio & Leek Pie

**Makes 1 large pie
or 6 small pies**

For the pastry

at least 2 batches savoury
shortcrust pastry (page 11)

For the filling

50g (1¾oz) salted butter

400g (14oz) leeks, trimmed
and finely sliced

1 tablespoon fresh thyme
leaves

250g (9oz) waxy potatoes,
quartered and sliced into
0.5cm (¼ in) slices

500ml (18fl oz) vegetable
stock

125g (4½oz) Taleggio,
chopped into 1cm (½in)
cubes

sea salt flakes and freshly
ground black pepper

For the sauce

50g (1¾oz) salted butter

2 tablespoons plain flour

100ml (3½fl oz) milk

1 teaspoon wholegrain
mustard (optional)

Variations and additions

• Add freshly ground black
  pepper to the pastry

• Add spices such as ground
  caraway or fennel seeds to
  the leek mixture.

I just adore Taleggio. It is a great melting cheese with a mild yet fruity flavour, and it works incredibly well with leeks. The secret here is to sauté the leeks in butter nice and slowly, so their natural sweetness is amplified and they remain uncoloured. The binding sauce is thick, as it should be, so the finished filling is oozing and soft. It's a real treat. If you can't find Taleggio, a ripe Brie or Morbier would also work.

Line your tin with one batch of the pastry and blind-bake and trim according to the instructions on page 13. Leave the baked pastry case in the tin for filling and finishing.

Heat a large saucepan over a low heat and add the butter, leeks, thyme and a good pinch of salt. Cover loosely with a piece of baking paper and allow to cook slowly until soft but not coloured – this shouldn't be rushed, taking up to 15 minutes. Stir from time to time to prevent the leeks from catching on the bottom of the pan.

Add the potatoes, along with a generous grinding of pepper, and stir to combine, then add the stock. Allow to simmer for around 20 minutes or until the potatoes are soft and the liquid has evaporated. Transfer to a bowl and set aside.

To make the sauce, add the butter and flour to the saucepan over a medium heat. Allow the butter to melt and the flour to sizzle for a minute, then pour in the milk, whisking continuously until thickened. Allow the sauce to bubble over a low heat for 5 minutes, then stir in the mustard (if using) and pour the sauce over the leek mixture. Allow to cool completely, then add the cubed Taleggio. Mix well so that everything is evenly distributed.

Fill the pre-baked pastry case almost to the top with the cheesy leeks, levelling off with a palette knife or similar. Top with your decorative pastry lid of choice and bake, according to the instructions on page 17.

To take advantage of the melting Taleggio this pie is best served hot, but do allow it to cool for 5 minutes before slicing.

Yin & Yang

Roll out your pastry platforms and mark out the working
areas (see page 14). Search online for a yin-yang symbol
and print it out at the size you want, then cut out to
create a template for cutting the pastry shapes. Arrange
these shapes on the pastry platform, then use discs
to frame the design. The discs were made using small
punch cutters.

Fringe

*Completely unplanned faffing led me here. There was no
specific inspiration source: it was just me, my pastry, my
music and my spaghetti cutter. I like it; it's different. I should
start to make notes of what is passing through my mind when
I create new things, to see if there is any connection between
the thought and the result.*

A reasonable amount of patience is required for this design.
The fringe effect is created by laying individual strips of
pastry side by side around the outside edge of the pie lid.
Mark out a circle by drawing around a plate using the back
of a knife. Brush the area where the fringe is to be laid with
egg wash, and cover with spaghetti pastry, see pages 34–35.
I cut-out circles from the base and added pastry discs to
finish the design.

Chess

Was it a floor or a chessboard that gave me the idea for this finish? I'm not really sure that either did. I'd be more inclined to say that it was because I cut out some pastry squares to play around with, and it evolved from there. With edible paint in hand, suddenly a chequered pie was before me.

To make the pastry tiles, consistently rolled pastry is key. Begin by hand-rolling your pastry, then cut it into wide strips. Pass these strips through the plain roller of a pasta machine, set to the widest setting. Now, use a pizza wheel to cut the pastry into squares. I use the width of a ruler as a guide, first cutting long strips, then turning the ruler and cutting the strips into squares. Use edible paint to colour the pastry. Paint half the pastry tiles and allow to dry. When ready to lay the tiles, brush the pastry platform (see page 14) with the egg wash and place the tiles in position, working slightly beyond the marked-out area. The edges can be neatened up when the lid is transferred to the pie.

Cherry & Custard Pie

**Makes 1 large pie
or 6 small pies**

For the pastry

at least 2 batches sweet
shortcrust pastry (page 10)

For the fruit filling

200g (7oz) fresh sweet
cherries, halved and stoned

30g (1oz) caster sugar

For the crème pâtissière

5 egg yolks

100g (3½oz) caster sugar

40g (1½oz) plain flour

425ml (15fl oz) full-fat milk

2 teaspoons vanilla bean
paste

Variations and additions

• Add citrus zest to the
pastry.

• Infuse the milk with
cinnamon or star anise
by heating together for
30 minutes, before
discarding the spices.

• Add a splash of almond
extract to the crème
pâtissière.

• Swap the cherries for the
soft fruit of your choice.

Use the biggest, juiciest, ripe cherries you can find for this pie. As they will be swamped in a thick custard, they need to be juicy enough to stand their ground. You could also use frozen cherries, but to be honest I found them to be a little underwhelming when testing.

Line your tin with one batch of the pastry and blind-bake and trim according to the instructions on page 13. Leave the baked pastry case in the tin for filling and finishing.

To prepare the fruit, combine the halved cherries and sugar in a bowl, stirring gently, then allow to macerate at room temperature while making the crème pâtissière.

To make the crème pâtissière, place the egg yolks and 3 tablespoons of the sugar in a large bowl. Whisk until the mixture is pale and has some volume. Add the flour and whisk to combine.

In a large saucepan over a medium heat, stir the milk, vanilla and remaining sugar together, removing the pan from the heat as soon as the mixture boils. Pour a little of the hot milk mixture over the egg yolks and mix well, then add the remainder while whisking continuously. Pour the resulting custard back into the pan and bring to a gentle boil. Allow the custard to bubble and thicken for about 2 minutes, whisking all the while. Once it has thickened and the raw flour has cooked, transfer the custard to a bowl, covering the surface with a layer of clingfilm before it cools to prevent a skin from forming. Allow to cool completely before use. When you're ready to use it, vigorously whisk the mixture until smooth.

Drain any excess juice from the cherries, keeping it for later. Cover the base of the pre-baked pastry case with the cut fruit. Use the crème pâtissière to blanket the cherries, either by piping or spooning it over. Fill the case almost to the top, then level off. Room for expansion is needed, as the custard puffs during baking. Spoon over any reserved cherry juice; making small holes in the custard to help it seep in, giving an extra boost of cherry flavour.

Top with your decorative pastry lid of choice and bake, according to the instructions on page 17.

During baking, remove from the oven every so often before returning again. This will prevent the custard from spilling over or pushing off the pie lid.

Mandalas

I lost both my mum and my stepdad within six months of each other, after which life naturally took a downward turn. The grief set in hard after losing Ged; I stopped looking after myself, the world suddenly seemed a lonely place to be in. I suppose I hit the self-destruct button, spending months spiralling into chaos and depression. There was, however, a pivotal moment, which brought me the awareness I needed: the realisation of how low I had become. I knew I needed help. I needed to heal. I found the help I needed in reiki. Both the power of the reiki and the lady who practised it upon me, undoubtedly changed my life, nudging me back onto the right track. My healing began. My experience with reiki inspired my first mandala pie, which was an interpretation of a chakra. I will always enjoy making these pie tops; I find the meditative placement of the design soothing.

I have a mandala colouring book, designed for spending mindful hours carefully colouring in. However, I don't use my book for that purpose: I use it for pastry templates instead! Cut out the main shape from a selected mandala and use as a template to cut out the pastry. Use push cutters to create symmetrical designs on the pastry platform (see page 14). All that's needed is imagination and careful placement. Cutting up the daisies will create lots of options (see page 108): halving them or using double or single petals creates lovely shapes.

Simple Symmetry

This is a more simplistic mandala than the one pictured on page 108, yet it is still effective.
Roll out a pastry platform and mark out your working area (see page 14), then use a variety
of cutters in different sizes to create the pattern, working around a central point. The
important thing is that the mandala is symmetrical. You can cut holes in the pastry: this
looks especially nice if the filling is colourful. I suggest chilling the pastry before cutting,
and find the small end of a plain piping nozzle to be perfect for the job.

Lily of the Valley

One of my favourite flowers, so delicate and pretty. I rented a house for a while with a garden that was bursting with flowers of all varieties. The planting had been carefully thought out so there was something new budding throughout the seasons. The lily of the valley was planted in a bed just outside the back door, their scent a welcoming beckon into the garden beyond.

First, roll out a pastry platform and mark out your working area (see page 14). Create templates for the leaves by hand-drawing onto paper and cutting them out. Use images from books as a guide, or actual leaves. Use the templates to cut out leaves from rolled pastry and arrange them on the pastry platform, bending and scoring with the back of a knife for extra detail and movement. The stems and roots of the flowers can be made using thin strips of pastry cut using the spaghetti cutter on a pasta machine. For the flowers, I used a small daisy push cutter, then wrapped the shape over a small ball of pastry. Arrange the flowers randomly, changing the direction in which they are positioned. Use edible glitter to highlight the flowerheads.

Bejewelled Earrings *(overleaf)*

This was one of the designs where I let impulse take over, allowing creativity to flow, not stopping until I was truly satisfied. Although I own lots of different-shaped pastry cutters, I didn't have anything elongated like the main shape used in the design, so I created the desired shape on my laptop, then printed and cut it out to use as a template for cutting the pastry.

To build up the design, first roll out a pastry platform and mark out the working area (see page 14). Arrange the shapes in your desired pattern, then (if you wish) decorate further using edible sprinkles. These will stay in place if pressed into the pastry, or a slight brushing of egg wash can be used to help glue them in place. Most sugar sprinkles will withstand the heat of the oven, but I can't personally guarantee every brand, so test a few first to be sure.

There is so much inspiration to be taken from jewellery. If I come across photographs of unusual pieces, I will save the image and file it away until I can think of a way to translate the intricate designs. This particular design was inspired by a spectacular pair of Nadia Morgenthaler earrings.

Chocolate Mousse Tart

**Makes 1 large tart
or 6 small tarts**

For the pastry

1 batch sweet shortcrust
pastry (page 10)

**For the chocolate mousse
filling**

200g (7oz) best-quality
dark chocolate (I like to use
one with 60–70 per cent
cocoa solids), broken into
small pieces, plus extra for
grating (optional)

125ml (4fl oz) milk

3 eggs, separated

60g (2¼oz) caster sugar

Variations and additions

- Add vanilla seeds or
orange zest to the pastry.

- Add a layer of fruit
beneath the mousse. This
will result in some leftover
mousse, which can be set
in a decorative glass for
a delicious dessert.

- Use your favourite
flavoured chocolate –
mint, orange or perhaps
chilli.

This was a favourite dessert during my years as a supper club host. The unexpected bubbly texture of the chocolate filling was always a talking point. It's great on its own, served with perfectly whipped cream, or you could hide hidden pockets of flavour underneath the mousse: my favourite option would be dark, sweet, liqueur-macerated cherries. Heaven.

This recipe does contain raw eggs, so use the freshest organic eggs you can find, or, if you prefer, you can use pasteurized egg yolks and whites; just use the quantity equivalents as suggested on the carton.

Line your tin with the pastry and blind-bake and trim according to the instructions on page 13. Leave the baked pastry case in the tin for filling and finishing. Any excess pastry can be used for decoration if you would like.

Place the chocolate in a heatproof bowl set over a pan of simmering water, ensuring that the base of the bowl is not in contact with the water. Add the milk to the bowl and allow the rising steam below to gently melt the chocolate. Stir every so often until the milk and the chocolate are combined and silky. Take off the heat and set aside to cool for a few minutes, then add the egg yolks, one at a time, stirring well between each addition.

In a separate, very clean bowl, make a meringue by whisking together the egg whites and sugar, either by hand or with an electric whisk, until stiff peaks form. The meringue should look glossy, but individual bubbles should be visible. Tip the bowl to one side: if the mixture slides about, whisk for a little longer; if it stays put, the meringue is ready.

Spoon a third of the egg whites into the bowl with the chocolate and whisk well. This will loosen up the chocolate, enabling you to fold in the rest easily without losing those all-important bubbles. Add another third, but this time fold it in gently. Then add the final third, again folding gently. When all is combined, with no streaks of white meringue visible, gently pour the mixture into the pre-baked tart case, holding the bowl as close to the tart case as possible. Gently shake the tart tin to level off the top.

continued overleaf

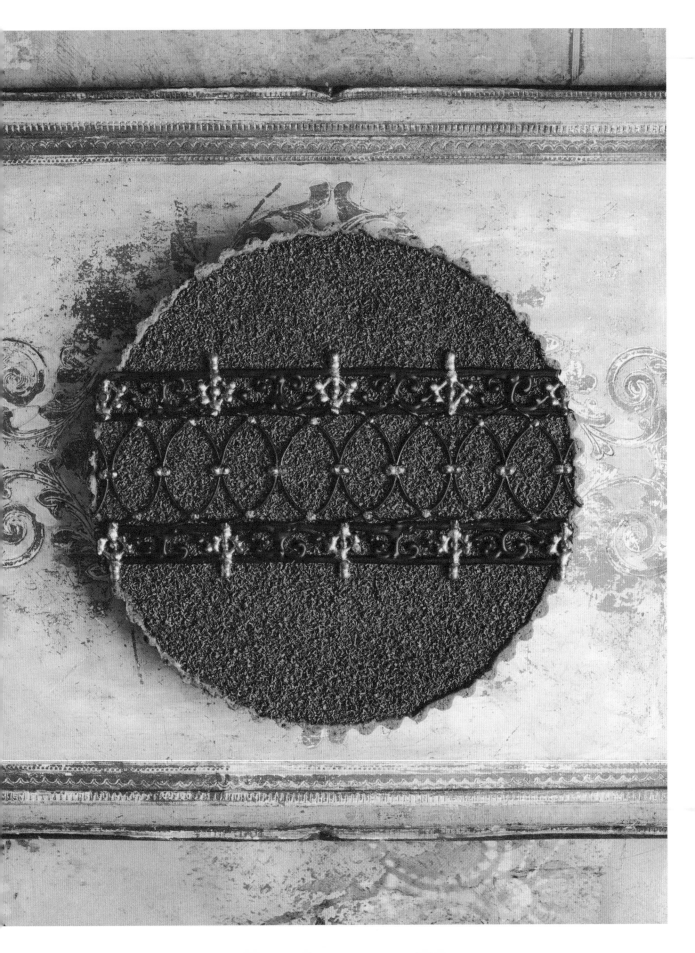

Transfer to the fridge for at least 2 hours to set, then decorate if desired. Remove from the tin just before serving, and use a heated blade to cut perfect slices. Allow to come up to room temperature before serving.

The tart can be kept in the fridge for up to 3 days, with little effect on the pastry, so with that in mind, you could make this up to 3 days in advance before serving.

Chocolate Railings

Patterns, symmetry and beautiful things are always around us: the art, creative vision and skill of others can be found everywhere. Next time you're out walking, take it all in. I remember on one particular day in Carlisle, I seemed to home in on railings: detailed and ornate and yet often walked past without a glance, ignored for the buildings behind them.

I made the chocolate railings using melted chocolate. I found an image of some railings that I liked online, then printed it off and used it as a template. Tape your printout to the work surface, then place a piece of non-stick baking paper over the top, taping that into position too. Melt some chocolate in a heatproof bowl and allow to cool slightly before transferring to a piping bag fitted with a plain nozzle. Pipe the chocolate onto the baking paper, tracing the pattern below. The consistency of the piping chocolate needs to be just right – not too fast-flowing and not too thick – so do experiment until the flow is controllable. Leave the design to solidify at room temperature, then transfer to the tart, gently peeling off the baking paper underneath. Apply some edible gold glitter with a small artist's brush to add a bit of luxury.

Crescent Flourishes

*I love antique furniture, as well as mirrors, picture frames...
anything overly ornate. It's my mum's style rubbing off
on me, I suppose. I have a few pieces of her furniture,
including a French-style sofa that has wooden arms and a
back carved with scrolled flourishes. I often sit on the sofa,
thinking of her running her hands over the carved arms,
just as I do now.*

These crescent flourishes were made and baked
separately, so create them upon baking paper. First, cut
out horseshoe shapes from hand-rolled pastry, then
use various push cutters to achieve the design on top.
I find that using a daisy cutter then cutting the shape
into individual petals is effective for intricate work. Pass
rolled-out pastry through the spaghetti cutter of a pasta
machine to make thin strips used to form the spirals.
Chill the crescents for at least 30 minutes before egg
washing and bake for 12–15 minutes, or until golden.

Fruit, Flowers & Butterflies

I made the chocolate butterflies by piping melted chocolate over a template. Again, the consistency of the piping chocolate needs to be just right, so keep testing until the flow is controllable. As with the chocolate railings on page 119, I printed off some butterfly images, taped the printout to the work surface and taped a piece of non-stick baking paper over the top, then piped the chocolate onto the baking paper, tracing the image underneath. Leave to solidify at room temperate, then transfer to the tart, gently peeling away the baking paper. If you want to add some pastry shapes, these can be cut and baked beforehand. Decorate the tart with some edible flowers and other fruit too.

Lime Tart

**Makes 1 large tart
or 6 small tarts**

For the pastry

at least 2 batches sweet
shortcrust pastry (page 10)

For the filling

5 eggs

300g (10½oz) condensed
milk

300ml (10fl oz) double
cream

zest of 4 limes and juice of 6
(about 200ml/7fl oz)

Variations and additions

- Add vanilla seeds to the
  pastry.
- Finish the tart with a layer
  of meringue.
- Infuse the cream with
  basil for a herbal note by
  heating together for 30
  minutes, before discarding
  the basil.

This zingy tart is great to have in your repertoire. It is surprisingly refreshing, even though it's laden with dairy. I love condensed milk in baking: it's sweet, thick and, for me, so nostalgic. I urge the sweet-toothed among you to spread some straight from the tin over hot buttered white toast (salted butter, naturally). So good!

This filling is a take on key lime pie, but I've used a sweet shortcrust pastry and focused on the lime filling. However, if you wanted to take the traditional route, create a base using crushed biscuits and melted butter, then top with meringue.

Line your tin with the pastry and blind-bake and trim according to the instructions on page 13. Leave the baked pastry case in the tin for filling and finishing. Any excess pastry can be used for decoration.

Preheat the oven to 140°C/120°C fan/275°F/gas mark 1.

Crack the eggs into a large bowl and beat together using a fork, trying not to incorporate too much air. Add the condensed milk and whisk together, then pour in the cream. Stir well, then add the lime zest and juice. Leave to sit for about 10 minutes, then pass the mixture through a fine sieve into a large jug for easy pouring.

Place the tin containing your blind-baked pastry case on a baking sheet. Remove all of the shelves from the oven except one, which should be positioned towards the bottom. Place the baking sheet and tin on this shelf, then pour the mixture into the pastry case. The space you've created by removing the other oven shelves will enable an easy pour, so you can fill right to the very top of the pastry case without having to move the tart. Bake for 20 minutes before checking; it will probably need a bit longer, but it's always a good idea to check at this point. I test by gently tapping the oven shelf with a wooden spoon, looking for movement across the surface. There should still be ripples of movement in the centre. If there are ripples towards the edges, bake for another 5 minutes and test again, bearing in mind that the tart will set further as it cools.

Remove from the oven and leave to cool, then allow to set fully in the fridge for a minimum of 2 hours before decorating and serving.

Open Flower Lattice

This open-cut tart-topper is made by cutting out shapes from a pastry disc. Roll the pastry relatively thickly (to prevent breakage), then cut into a circle the same size as the tart. I recommend chilling the pastry disc well to make the cutting process easier. Cut out shapes using daisy and circular push cutters. Chill well, then bake at 200°C/180°C fan/400°F/gas mark 6 for about 20 minutes until golden. Cut out and bake extra pastry flowers, which can be positioned afterwards, along with some tiny edible petals, if wanted.

Chocolate Fronds & Edible Leaves

Print off some leaf templates and tape the printout to your work surface. Tape some non-stick baking paper over the top and pipe over melted chocolate, tracing the shape underneath (see page 119). Allow to solidify at room temperature, then carefully transfer from the paper to the tart. The use of some attractive edible leaves and petals will complete the look.

NATURE

I am heavily inspired by nature. It only takes a short stroll outside and there will be something to catch my eye. A feather, some flowers, some tangled leaves, a butterfly floating past, or perhaps a magnificent tree standing alone and proud within a field.

My mum had a gorgeous garden, full to the brim with shrubs and flowers, bursting with colour, especially in May. People would stop and admire her azaleas as they walked past. I am not remotely green-fingered, but I do have a real passion for flowers, something my mum assured me I'd have when I was older. I confess that at the time I much preferred to admire flowers printed on fabrics or wallpaper, and my love of real flowers only developed in recent years. Before I would have walked past a bloom, not even taking a sideways glance. Now I will cross a road to look closer if something catches my eye, investigating and taking photographs, wondering if I can recreate the form in pastry. I will never tire of dahlias, wisteria, lupins and delphiniums, and I have made pastry versions of them all.

As well as flowers and leaves; insects and feathers have inspired me to create too, the feathers and the butterfly pies both holding a special meaning, as well as being fundamentally inspired by nature they also symbolize life. The butterfly (page 73) I made to signify a new start; the feathers (page 96) I recreated after my mum passed. White feathers would bring me great comfort in the months that followed, little signs that told me she was still with me.

Next time you're out walking, look out for an inspiring bloom, a flash of colour or something floating on the breeze. Allow yourself to absorb and be inspired by the nature that is around you. It could be the shape of a leaf, a cluster of wild flowers or the way the sun is reflecting on the water. All can be interpreted somehow, in your own way.

Milk Tart

**Makes 1 large tart
or 6 small tarts**

For the pastry

1 batch sweet shortcrust
pastry (page 10)

For the filling

5 egg yolks, beaten

160g (5¾oz) caster sugar

¼ teaspoon fine salt

2 tablespoons cornflour

1½ tablespoons plain flour

450ml (16fl oz) milk

150ml (5fl oz) double cream

35g (1¼oz) cold unsalted
butter, grated (optional)

Variations and additions

• Add ground cinnamon to
the pastry or dust the top
of the tart with ground
cinnamon or ground
nutmeg.

• Infuse the milk with
aromatic spices – for
example cardamom, star
anise and cinnamon – by
heating together for 30
minutes, before discarding
the spices.

I'm all for a tart that allows for artistic faffing: a blank canvas on which you can lay all kinds of extra decoration, be that petals, dustings of cinnamon or pastry overlays. The only limit is your imagination. Custard tart, panna cotta tart and lemon tart are all perfect examples of a 'blank canvas' baking scenario, as is this traditional South African *melktart*. Not only is it perfect for decor, this sweet treat is also the ultimate comfort food for all ages. The thickened milk filling is made on the hob and requires no oven time, but it's important to allow plenty of cooling time for the tart to set fully before decorating and slicing.

Line your tin with the pastry and blind-bake and trim according to the instructions on page 13. Leave the baked pastry case in the tin for filling and finishing.

In a bowl, vigorously whisk together the egg yolks, sugar, salt, cornflour and flour, then set aside.

Pour the milk and cream into a large saucepan over a low heat and heat very gently. As the mixture reaches boiling point, remove from the heat and pour a little into the egg mixture in the bowl, mixing well. This will temper the egg yolks. Now pour in the rest and whisk well.

Wash out the pan, then pour the custard mixture through a sieve back into the clean pan. Set over a low–medium heat and whisk continuously for 2–3 minutes until thickened. As the mixture heats up, the flours will cook out and thicken the liquid in the process. Add the grated butter, if using, and whisk to combine. The butter will add an extra richness, making the custard a little silkier.

Sieve into a large jug for easy pouring, then pour it into the pre-baked tart case, while still hot. Gently shake the tart tin so the mixture levels off well; you could use a palette knife to smooth off further if you wish. Allow the tart to cool fully, then place in the fridge for a minimum of 2 hours to set before decorating and serving.

Edible Petal Waves

The inspiration for the waves of colour on this tart came from a stunning dress I saw in a magazine. The wave-like pattern and blocks of colour appealed to me; the idea translated well.

I used lots of organic edible flower petals to make the floral waves, which look pretty against the milk filling. Mark out the wave first with the back of a knife and simply fill in the spaces with the petals; these were dahlias.

Cocoa Dusting

Traditionally, milk tarts are completely covered with a thick layer of ground cinnamon, but I felt the contrasting colour beneath was calling out to be seen. Any cut-out could be used, but my love of butterflies made those the obvious choice.

This is such a simple yet effective way to decorate a tart. Find some butterfly templates online and print them off, then cut them out and lay them on the surface of the tart. After a heavy dusting of cocoa, remove the paper templates, revealing the contrasting colour below.

Open-cut Lattice

I will always be in awe of architectural design, especially work found in churches, cathedrals and places of worship. As well as the stunning carvings and stonework, I take great inspiration from the ceilings of such places: endless beauty, imagination and artistry brought to life by mind-boggling feats of engineering. There is so much inspiration to be found – always look up!

The open-cut lattice was made from rolled-out pastry (rolled relatively thick, to prevent breakage), which was cut and baked separately. I suggest freezing the pastry disc before cutting the shapes from it, and carefully calculating where to cut for a slick finish. The balls inside each cut-out were made by using a small push cutter then rolling the pastry in the palm of my hand. They are held in place with a dab of egg wash. Reinforce the rim of the disc with strips of pastry, cut using the tagliatelle cutter on a pasta machine. Chill well before baking, then bake at 200°C/180°C fan/400°F/gas mark 6 for about 20 minutes until golden. Finish with a dusting of edible glitter.

Sweet Pumpkin Tart

**Makes 1 large tart
or 6 small tarts**

For the pastry

1 batch sweet shortcrust
pastry (page 10)

For the filling

750g (1lb 10oz) pumpkin,
seeds removed but skin on,
cut into rough 5cm (2in)
chunks

2 tablespoons vegetable oil

250g (9oz) condensed milk

½ teaspoon ground
cinnamon

¼ teaspoon ground cloves

½ teaspoon ground ginger

¼ teaspoon ground allspice

4 eggs

Variations and additions

• Add vanilla seeds to the
  pastry.

• Change up the spice blend
  to suit your personal taste.

• Serve decorated with
  whipped cream.

Instead of using canned pumpkin purée, this delicious tart involves roasting a fresh pumpkin or squash to tenderness. The difference in the flavour and texture is far superior. My favourite pumpkin to use is the Delicia, which has the most amazing colour and sweet-tasting flesh. The velvety-smooth, buttery, intense sweetness blows my mind every time I taste it – do source one if you can. Good alternatives are the Kent and Kabocha varieties, but butternut squash will work brilliantly.

Line your tin with the pastry and blind-bake and trim according to the instructions on page 13. Leave the baked pastry case in the tin for filling and finishing. Any excess pastry can be used for decoration.

Preheat the oven to 200°C/180°C fan/400°F/gas mark 6

Place the pumpkin chunks in a deep roasting tray and drizzle with the oil, tossing to coat. Roast for 1 hour, then cover with foil and continue to roast for another 30 minutes. You are looking for slightly caramelized, tender flesh. Once done, remove from the oven and leave to cool in the tray.

When cool enough to handle, spoon the pumpkin flesh from the skin, discarding the skin and any overly charred bits. Ideally, you should end up with about 350g (12¼oz) flesh, but don't worry too much if the weight is slightly under. Put the pumpkin flesh in a food processor. Add the condensed milk and all of the spices then pulse until smooth and silky. Transfer to a large bowl, making sure to transfer every last drop.

In a separate bowl, beat the eggs (without incorporating too much air), then stir them into the pumpkin mixture. Pass through a fine sieve.

Reduce the oven temperature to 140°C/120°C fan/275°F/gas mark 1.

Place the tin containing your blind-baked pastry case on a baking sheet and pour the pumpkin mixture into the case, filling it as close to the top of the pastry case as possible. Bake for 35 minutes, then check by gently tapping the oven shelf with a wooden spoon, looking for movement across the surface. There should be ripples towards the centre. If there are ripples moving towards the edges, leave to bake for a bit longer, checking every 5 minutes. The filling will set further as it cools, so don't be tempted to overbake. When done, remove from the oven and leave to cool completely before decorating.

Butterflies & Flowers *(page 130)*

A selection of edible flowers and leaves, along with some pre-baked pastry shapes, fruit and sprinkles, can make any sweet tart prettier. When placing the decorations, try to do so without overthinking: the more natural the placement, the more beautiful the finish will be.

Baked Pastry Tiles *(opposite)*

Pre-baked pastry shapes make for effective decor. The shapes, of course, can differ, as can the way in which they are arranged. Here, I opted for triangles, which were cut using a triangular cutter. (If you don't have a triangle cutter, simply mark out equilateral triangles on strips of pastry, then cut.) Chill the cut pastry well before baking, then egg wash and bake at 200°C/180°C fan/400°F/gas mark 6 for 10 minutes until golden and crisp. The baked tiles can be arranged upon the tart's surface. A little trimming may be required to make some edges fit, in which case I recommend using a serrated knife.

Baked White Chocolate Tarts

**Makes 6 small tarts
or 1 large tart**

For the pastry

1 batch sweet shortcrust
pastry (page 10)

For the filling

5 egg yolks

1 tablespoon caster sugar

350ml (11¾fl oz) double
cream

1 teaspoon vanilla bean
paste

175g (6¼oz) white chocolate
(at least 28 per cent cocoa
solids), chopped

Variations and additions

- Add vanilla seeds to the
  pastry.

- Infuse the cream with
  cardamom pods (5 would
  be a good number to try)
  by heating together for 30
  minutes, before discarding
  the pods.

- Top the cooled tarts with
  sugar and brûlée them for
  crunch.

- Swap the white chocolate
  for milk chocolate.

This is truly one of the best tart fillings you'll ever make. The soft set white chocolate custard is beyond heavenly: it's sweet, comforting and rewarding. I have never encountered anyone who doesn't enjoy this dessert. It was always a huge hit during my supper club years, and is perfect for any occasion. If needed, the sweetness can be counterbalanced with some tart fruit, such as roasted rhubarb or perhaps some redcurrants.

Line six individual tins with the pastry and blind-bake and trim according to the instructions on page 13. Leave the baked pastry cases in the tin for filling and finishing. Any excess pastry can be used for decoration.

Preheat the oven to 130°C/110°C fan/265°F/gas mark ¾ (I suggest you use an oven thermometer).

In a bowl, use an electric whisk to vigorously whisk together the egg yolks and sugar for 1 minute until thickened.

In a large saucepan over a medium heat, stir the cream and vanilla together, removing the pan from the heat as soon as the mixture boils. Pour a little of the hot cream onto the egg yolks and whisk, then add a splash more and whisk again. Add the remaining cream, followed by the chopped white chocolate, and stir slowly, allow the heat to melt the chocolate. Pour through a fine sieve into a large jug for easy pouring.

Place the tins containing your blind-baked pastry cases on a baking sheet. Remove all the shelves from the oven except one, which should be positioned towards the bottom. Put the baking sheet with the tart cases on the shelf, then pour the custard mixture into the cases. The space you've created above by removing the other shelves means you can pour with ease and control, preventing spillage. Fill it as close to the top of the pastry cases as possible. Bake for 15 minutes (25 if making a single, larger tart); they may need a bit longer, but do check at this point. Test by gently tapping the oven shelf with a wooden spoon, looking for movement across the surface of the tarts. There should be ripples towards the centre. If the ripples are moving towards the edges, bake for another 5–15 minutes, checking every 5 minutes. The tarts will set further as they cool, so don't be tempted to overbake.

Edible Petals

Whenever using flowers, do make sure they are indeed edible and source them from an organic grower. Some flowers can taste quite peppery and overpowering, so do bear this in mind with your selection.

Antique Flourishes

I made the flourishes by printing off templates found online. There are endless options, so choose which you like best. First print off the image and cut out carefully, then use that as a guide for cutting the shape from rolled-out pastry. I enhanced the shapes further by building up some detail, adding strips of pastry along with circular cut-outs. Chill well prior to baking, then bake at 200°C/180°C fan/400°F/gas mark 6 for about 15 minutes until golden. Use edible glitter to finish, for a more antiqued look.

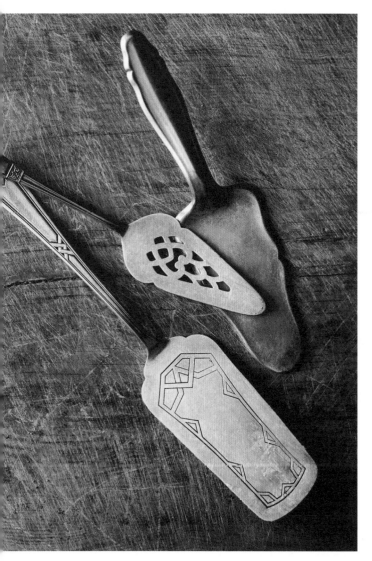

Meat
& Fish

Chicken, Tarragon & Leek Pie

**Makes 1 large pie
or 6 small pies**

For the pastry

at least 2 batches savoury
shortcrust pastry (page 11)

For poaching the chicken

1.5kg (3lb 5oz) whole
chicken, preferably free-
range and organic

1 large carrot, finely sliced,
200g (7oz) prepped weight

2 celery sticks, finely sliced,
125g (4½oz) prepped weight

1 onion, finely sliced, 125g
(4½oz) prepped weight

2 tarragon sprigs

2 teaspoons fine salt

8 black peppercorns

1 teaspoon fennel seeds
(optional)

For the filling

50ml (2fl oz) olive oil

40g (1½oz) butter

1 onion, finely sliced, 125g
(4½oz) prepped weight

1 large leek, trimmed and
sliced, 200g (7oz) prepped
weight

2 tablespoons plain flour

2 tarragon sprigs, leaves
picked and chopped

125ml (4fl oz) double cream

sea salt flakes and freshly
ground black pepper

1 tablespoon Dijon mustard

There are so many ways to prepare chicken for a pie. Frying and roasting are both perfectly good methods, and each will bring different characteristics to the finished filling. Here I've opted to poach a whole chicken, along with aromatic vegetables, herbs and spices, to give both a deliciously juicy chicken and a perfect stock for the sauce. Use the best chicken you can: the flavour, texture and overall finish will be worth the extra spent.

Line your tin with one batch of the pastry and blind-bake and trim according to the instructions on page 13. Leave the baked pastry case in the tin for filling and finishing.

Place the chicken and all the poaching ingredients in a large pan over a medium heat and cover with cold water. Bring to the boil, then reduce to a slow simmer. Poach the chicken for 45 minutes, or until cooked through. Remove the chicken from the poaching liquid and set aside on a plate to cool. Increase the heat back to medium and reduce the cooking liquid by half. Measure out 125ml (4fl oz) of the stock to use for the sauce and save the remainder for other recipes. It will keep in the fridge for 3 days, or you can freeze it – definitely don't waste it.

To make the filling, melt the oil and butter in a large frying pan over a low heat. Add the sliced onion and leek, along with a little salt, and sauté for 10 minutes until softened. Increase the heat to medium, then add the flour and stir everything well for 1 minute until the flour cooks out. Add the reserved cooking stock, then stir and simmer for a few minutes until thickened, adding a few twists of pepper if wanted. Take off the heat.

Strip the meat from the chicken, discarding the skin. Be sure to get the oysters (two oval pieces of dark meat either side of the backbone), and all of the thick thigh meat (the tastiest parts). You will only need one of the breasts, so save the other for use in another meal. Shred or chop the meat into small bite-sized pieces and add them to the pan, along with the chopped tarragon. Stir in the cream, then allow the mixture to cool completely.

Fill the pre-baked pastry case almost to the top, levelling off with a palette knife. Top with your pastry lid of choice and bake, following the guidelines on page 17.

This pie is best served hot from the oven, although allow to cool for a few minutes before slicing.

Folies Bergère

Although I have never been to the Folies Bergère, the famous cabaret hall in Paris, I am aware of the golden art deco piece by Maurice Picaud that crowns its doorway. This pie was inspired by that very artwork, minus the naked lady! Building up the different shapes and textures on this pie felt quite different to anything I'd ever done before, and as the golden edible glitter is flavourless, I felt I could really go for it.

It appears I have thrown everything but the kitchen sink at this pie top, creativity in full flow. I used lots of different techniques, including a little area of parquet (see page 70 for full instructions) and special cutters for the wavy sections (pictured on page 206). In other parts I framed circles and rectangles with thin strips of pastry cut using the spaghetti attachment of a pasta machine. If you want to recreate this pie top, or something similar, I suggest having lots of cutters on hand and just going with what feels right.

Mark out the working area on your pastry platform (see page 14) and arrange the design as you wish, using egg wash to hold everything in position. Finish by brushing with edible gold glitter. See page 141 for the entire, unbaked design.

Greek Earrings

Small oval push cutters were used to make up the majority of this design, laying the pieces alongside thin strips of pastry, which were cut using the spaghetti cutter of a pasta machine. Roll out the pastry platform and mark out your working area (see page 14), then build up the design as desired, using egg wash to hold everything in place.

Leek Flowers

Nature will always be a huge source of inspiration for me, flowers especially, as they're so perfect in their form and beauty. As the pie filling contains leek, their flowers seemed an obvious pastry decoration. They're so pretty: tall, proud stems with a wonderful pompom of tiny purple or white buds opening up like hundreds of stars.

Roll out a pastry platform and mark out the working area (see page 14). Hand-roll the stems of the flowers and hand-cut the leaves from rolled-out pastry. Indent the pastry with a circular cutter and build the flowerheads within these circles. Use a 5-point star cutter to create the tiny flowers, creating plenty to replicate the form of the allium flowerhead. After positioning the tiny flowers, use the point of a cocktail stick to push them into place. The purple sprinkles were made of sugar, so if adding these do bear this in mind, as they will bring a hint of sweetness to the finished pie. The design is pretty enough without the sprinkles, so they aren't essential.

Ham Hock, Mustard & Herb Pie

HAM

**Makes 1 large pie
or 6 small pies**

For the pastry

at least 2 batches savoury
shortcrust pastry (page 11)

For poaching the ham

1 ham hock joint, smoked if
preferred, about 1.5kg (3lb
5oz)

8 whole black peppercorns

3 dried bay leaves

4 thyme sprigs

1 carrot, very finely sliced,
125g (4½oz) prepped weight

1 onion, very finely sliced,
125g (4½oz) prepped weight

1 or 2 celery sticks, very
finely sliced, 85g (3oz)
prepped weight

For the filling

30g (1oz) salted butter

40g (1½oz) plain flour

3 teaspoons English
mustard

large handful of chopped
fresh herbs of your choice

sea salt flakes and freshly
ground black pepper

Variations and additions

• Add mustard powder
to the pastry.

• Add grated nutmeg or
some cheese to the sauce.

My mum would often boil up a ham hock to be used for sandwiches or to stir through soups and broths, or she would slice it up to serve alongside homemade chips and a fried egg. The very thought of these dishes makes me want to heat up the chip pan and get back to basics. Simple meals like these are perhaps the ones we remember the most. This pie filling, although it takes a bit more work, is extremely delicious and worth the effort.

If you do make this pie, it might be an idea to add an extra hock to the pan, use one for the pie filling and the other to slice up and use as described above.

Line your tin with one batch of the pastry and blind-bake and trim according to the instructions on page 13. Leave the baked pastry case in the tin for filling and finishing.

Place the ham hock in a large saucepan over a medium heat, adding enough cold water to completely cover it. Add the peppercorns, herbs and vegetables and bring to the boil, then reduce to a simmer. As the water heats up, some frothy bits may appear; simply use a slotted spoon to skim these off and discard, repeating until the water is clear. Cover the pan with a lid and simmer for 2½ hours, turning the ham occasionally. The time will vary depending on the size of the hock. The meat is ready when it comes away easily from the bone. Take off the heat and leave to cool in the stock for an hour, then transfer to a plate to cool completely. Strain the stock through a colander, discarding the vegetables, herbs and peppercorns, reserving the liquid to use for the sauce.

To make the filling, melt the butter in a clean pan over a medium heat until frothy, then stir in the flour. Measure out 300ml (10fl oz) of the ham stock. Pour about a third of it into the pan with the flour and butter mixture, whisking well. Once it thickens, add some more stock and continue whisking, adding more until the full amount has been incorporated. Stir in the mustard and herbs and allow to cool.

Pick the ham from the bone. Discard the thick, gelatinous skin, but do keep some of the fat that sits just below it (if you like it, that is); I think it adds an extra depth of flavour. Chop or strip the meat into bite-sized pieces and add to the sauce, stirring well to coat.

continued overleaf

Fill the pre-baked pastry case almost to the top with the ham mixture and level off with a palette knife. Top with your decorative pastry lid of choice and bake, according to the instructions on page 17.

I prefer to serve this pie hot, but do allow it to cool for 5 minutes before serving.

Four Feathers

When my lovely mum passed, her long battle with dementia finally taking her, she stayed with me for a while longer in the form of feathers. You've probably heard of this before, and perhaps even felt cynical about it, but whatever your thoughts, there's no other way that I can explain the feathers that floated alongside me as I walked, for months after she left me behind. While I don't see those floating feathers any more, they were the inspiration behind my pastry versions. My feather-topped pies will always be special to me, and I make them for the people I love, and for those special meals in life.

First roll out a pastry platform and mark out your working area (see page 14). Use a pasta roller to make the pastry feathers by passing wide strips through the plain roller, set to the widest setting, then cut those using the spaghetti roller. To make the feather shape, search online for feather templates and print out your favourite, then cut it out to use as a template to cut feathers from rolled-out pastry. Lay these feather shapes on the pastry platform, and brush with egg wash. Using the spaghetti strips, first lay a central spine down the middle of the feathers, then lay strips side by side on either side of that to replicate the feathers' strands. There's no need to measure the strips; just lay them down, then pull to break. Add a second layer of strips – not too many this time, just enough to create some 'movement' by placing the strands in slightly different directions. Finish with some edible glitter.

Pulled Pork & Apple Pie

**Makes 1 large pie
or 6 small pies**

For the pastry

at least 2 batches savoury
shortcrust pastry (page 11)

For the filling

1.5kg (3lb 5oz) pork
shoulder, skin removed but
fat below it left in place

2 tablespoons runny honey

2 teaspoons caraway seeds,
toasted and crushed

3 Cox apples, peeled, cored
and cut into large chunks

1 onion, peeled and sliced

4 fresh thyme sprigs

300ml (10fl oz) pork or
chicken stock

300ml (10fl oz) dry cider

large handful of fresh flat-
leaf parsley, chopped

splash of cider vinegar, to
taste

1 tablespoon wholegrain
mustard

sea salt flakes and freshly
ground black pepper

Variations and additions

- Use butternut squash in
  place of the apples.

- Use fennel or mustard
  seeds instead of caraway.

- Use horseradish sauce
  instead of mustard.

Slow-roasting a pork shoulder joint will leave you with succulent, tender meat that can be pulled apart with minimum effort. After the initial prep, there really is nothing much to do other than wait until the pork is cooked to melting tenderness, so use that cooking time to create a stunning pie top! There will be leftover filling, but you can use it to fill rolls for a delicious lunch, or freeze for another time.

Line your tin with one batch of the pastry and blind-bake and trim according to the instructions on page 13. Leave the baked pastry case in the tin for filling and finishing.

Preheat the oven to 160°C/140°C fan/325°F/gas mark 1.

Rub the surface of the pork with the honey: it's probably easiest to do this using your hands. Season well with salt and pepper and sprinkle over the caraway seeds.

Select a casserole dish that will hold the pork snugly, with only a little room around it. Arrange the chopped apples, onion and thyme sprigs in the dish, then rest the pork on top. Pour the stock and cider down the sides of the dish, then cover with the lid and place in the oven for up to 3½ hours. Check on it from time to time, topping up with a little water if the liquid seems to be reducing too much.

After 3½ hours (or when the pork is falling-apart tender), remove the pork and spoon the apples and onions out of the casserole dish, setting them aside. Return the meat to the dish and baste well with the juice. Increase the oven temperature to 240°C/220°C fan/475°F/gas mark 9. Once it has come up to temperature, return the pork to the oven, uncovered, for 15 minutes to gain some colour. Remove from the oven and allow to rest for 30 minutes before shredding. Reserve some juice.

Transfer the shredded meat to a large bowl and pour over 100ml (3½fl oz) of the remaining juice from the casserole dish. Add the apples, onion and chopped parsley and stir, then taste. Add the vinegar, mustard, and salt and pepper as needed to balance the flavours. Allow to cool fully.

Once cool, fill the pre-baked pastry case almost to the top with the pie filling and level off with a palette knife. Top with your decorative pastry lid of choice and bake, according to the instructions on page 17.

This pie is best served warm. Allow to cool for 5 minutes before slicing.

Ginkgo

I am lucky enough the travel the country, teaching and sharing my skills with fellow pastry enthusiasts, and one of my favourite cities to teach in is Bath. It is crammed with the most amazing architecture and history, but equally wonderful is its botanical garden. A slow stroll through those gardens is enough to fill you with inspiration for months to come. Last summer, I sat under a magnificent ginkgo tree watching the world go by, the sun shining through the leaves, casting shadows at my feet. It was a happy day.

The ginkgo has such beautifully shaped leaves. To recreate the shape perfectly, print off and cut out a template in various sizes, and use to cut the pastry. Make the branches and leaf stems using strips cut using the tagliatelle and spaghetti cutters of a pasta machine, hand-shape and indent the little buds with a wooden skewer. Use the back of a knife for the detailing on the leaves. Use edible paint to colour the decorations, using a small artist's brush for accuracy.

Chequerboard, Herringbone & Brick Parquet

Any parquet design requires accurate cutting of the pastry tiles. To fit together perfectly, they need to be cut in accordance with the pattern you want to use, so a little planning and some simple calculations are needed. I suggest using a pasta roller to give consistent and perfectly rolled pastry. Roll first by hand, then cut into wide strips and pass these through the plain roller of the pasta machine, set to the widest setting. Use a ruler and a small, sharp kitchen knife to mark out the measurements. I find a pizza wheel and a ruler are the best tools for cutting the tiles.

Have a pastry platform ready, with your working area marked out (see page 14). Using egg wash and an artist's brush, gently coat small areas of the pastry top and start laying the tiles in your chosen style. Continue until the working area is covered, going slightly over the edges; any excess can be trimmed off later.

Flower Trellis

This design actually started off as a window, but then went off track with flowers and leaves. I love it when flashes of inspiration strike and something new appears. To create your own version, roll out a pastry platform and mark out your working area (see page 14). Work out the positioning of the trellis and create it using strips of pastry. These strips could cut by hand or by using the tagliatelle cutter on a pasta machine. Use tear-shaped cutters to create the leaves, adding details with the back of a knife. Circular and daisy push cutters add detail. To create the thin flower stems, use the spaghetti cutter on a pasta machine. Use egg wash to hold all the details in place. See page 151 for the full design.

Scotch(ish) Pie

**Makes 1 large pie
or 6 small pies**

For the pastry

at least 2 batches savoury
shortcrust pastry (page 11)

For the filling

400g (14oz) mutton mince,
if possible (ask a butcher); if
not, use lamb mince

2 teaspoons freshly ground
black pepper

½ teaspoon ground mace

1½ teaspoon ground nutmeg

1 teaspoon fine salt

100ml (3½fl oz) lamb stock

Variations and additions

• Add some herbs of your
choice to the meat filling.

I developed my love of Scotch pies when I lived just over the Scottish border in Gretna as a child, and we were served them for school lunch a couple of times a month. I always eagerly anticipated Scotch pie days, and I'll never forget the peppery heat and the heavy use of spices within the meat. Truly delicious. If I ever see a tray of Scotch pies in a bakery or a butcher's shop window, I'm in, through the door and ordering one for immediate consumption! Traditionally, Scotch pies are made using hot water pastry rather than the shortcrust used here, so of course you could do that if you prefer.

Line your tin with one batch of the pastry and blind-bake and trim according to the instructions on page 13. Leave the baked pastry case in the tin for filling and finishing.

Making the filling really is just a case of bringing all the ingredients together: there's no pre-cooking needed. In a large bowl, crumble up the minced meat, then sprinkle over the spices, salt and stock and mix together well. Lifting the mince up with a light touch and sprinkling it back into the bowl will prevent the meat becoming a solid mass. Do this repeatedly until the spices and salt are mixed right through, then rest in the fridge for an hour. That's it. Easiest pie filling ever. It is now ready to be used.

Fill the pre-baked pastry case, almost to the top with the mince mixture and level off the top with a palette knife. Top with your decorative pastry lid of choice.

Preheat the oven to 200°C/180°C fan/400°F/gas mark 6.

As the meat filling isn't pre-cooked like the other recipes in this book, the baking time will take a longer. What you don't want is overbaked pastry and undercooked meat, so a little care is needed. Initially bake in the oven for 45 minutes (30 for individual pies) then check. The meat will not be cooked through at this point, but the pastry top may be starting to colour, more so in certain areas. A simple turn of the pie might be all that's needed, or perhaps cover completely with tin foil, to protect the pastry while the meat filling cooks through. Be attentive during the next 15 minutes, checking both pastry and the temperature of the filling every 5 minutes. I use a metal skewer to feel if the meat is piping hot in the middle, you may want to use a digital probe, which should read a minimum of 70°C (158°F) for 2 minutes. Allow to cool slightly before slicing.

This pie is as delicious cold as it is hot.

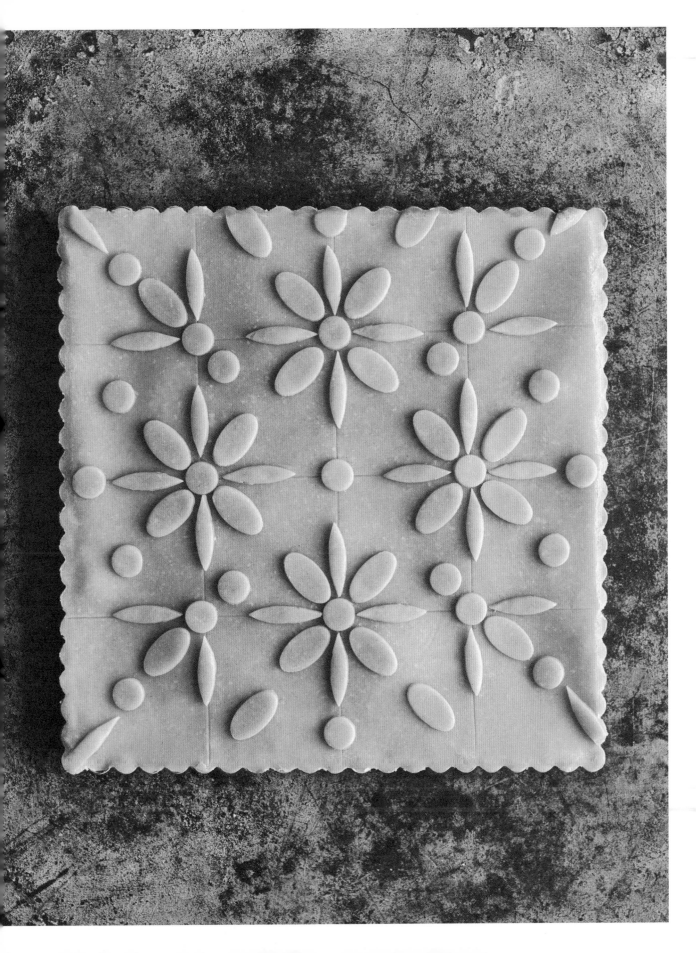

Antique Glass

I have an old sideboard that used to belong to my mum. She gave it to me when I first moved into what became my marital home. I love it, but I also love the treasures that it holds: lots of cut-crystal glasses of various sizes, shapes and patterns. Some were my mum's; some were my nana's; some were found at car-boot sales or second-hand shops, or given to me by friends. I use them all. They aren't hidden away and saved for best; I don't believe in that. Each time I use them, I take a moment to admire the patterns.

A very simple design that requires little explanation. Simply lay the cut-out pastry pieces on your pastry platform, working within a marked-out area (see page 14). If you want it to be really accurate, find the centre point and build the pattern from there.

Leaves

I think leaves will forever be a favourite decoration of mine. Where I used to use a leaf-shaped push cutter, I now prefer to make my own leaves using a tear-shaped cutter and marking the detail myself with the back of a knife. Adding stems and berries between the leaves will give extra interest. Simply lay your leaf patterns on your rolled-out pastry platforms, working within the marked-out area (see page 14) and use egg wash to hold everything in place.

Spirals

These spirals will take a bit of care and patience if you want them to be very neat. First, roll out a pastry platform and mark out your working area (see page 14). Then use the spaghetti cutter on a pasta machine to cut out long strips of pastry. Brush the pastry platform with a little egg wash, then curl up the end of a thin strip and place it on the platform before carefully coiling the rest of the strip around it, creating a spiral. Repeat all over the surface of the pastry, varying the sizes of the spirals. Fill in any gaps with pastry discs; finish with some metallic sprinkles if you like. These will add tiny bursts of sweetness to the finished pie, so do leave these off if that's something you would rather not have; pastry balls could always be used instead.

Oxtail & Shin Pie

**Makes 1 large pie
or 6 small pies**

For the pastry

At least 2 batches savoury
shortcrust pastry (page 11)

For the filling

1kg (2lb 4 oz) oxtail, cut into
sections (ask your butcher)

300g (10½oz) beef shin or
skirt thickly sliced

100ml vegetable oil, for
frying

200g (7oz) button
mushrooms, thinly sliced

100g (3½oz) celery, thinly
sliced

100g (3½oz) carrots, thinly
sliced

5 fresh thyme sprigs

200g (7oz) onions, thinly
sliced

1 star anise

200ml (7fl oz) red wine

1.5 litres (2¾ pints) beef
stock

2 dried bay leaves

400g (14oz) can chopped
tomatoes

1 teaspoon double-
concentrated tomato purée

sea salt flakes and freshly
ground black pepper

This is one of the best fillings in the book, in my opinion. Not only is it amazing encased in pastry, it can also be used as a rich ragu to top a saffron risotto, or cooked in a cottage pie. Admittedly, it's quite a lengthy process, involving preparation, cooking, cooling and bringing together, so you might like to start the day before you want to assemble the pie – but trust me, it's worth it.

Line your tin with one batch of the pastry and blind-bake and trim according to the instructions on page 13. Leave the baked pastry case in the tin for filling and finishing.

To make the filling, season the oxtail and beef shin with salt and pepper. Heat two tablespoons of the oil in a large frying pan over a high heat. Working in batches, brown the meat for around 10 minutes; you want it to sear rather than stew. Set aside on a plate, then season and fry the mushrooms in the same pan, again working in batches. Cook each batch for around 15 minutes until the mushrooms take on a caramel colour. Remove from the pan and drain on a plate lined with kitchen paper.

Add another two tablespoons of the oil to the pan, then add the celery and carrots, seasoning with some salt and pepper and the thyme. Fry for 15 minutes or until soft and starting to colour. Remove from the pan and drain on the same plate as the mushrooms. Finally, add the remaining oil to the pan and tip in the onions, along with the star anise (this intensifies meat flavours). Season with some salt and pepper and fry for around 30 minutes or until the onions are softened and caramelized. Remove from the pan. Deglaze the pan with the red wine, then to reduce to one-third of its volume.

Put all the vegetables and meat in a large saucepan, along with the stock, bay leaves, the canned tomatoes and the tomato purée. Place over a medium heat and bring to the boil, then reduce the heat to low and simmer for up to 4 hours. Check the level of liquid every so often and top up with water if the meat is exposed.

It's ready when the shin (or skirt) meat falls apart easily, and the oxtail meat falls from the bone with ease. Take off the heat and allow everything to cool in the pan. When the meat is cool enough to handle, drain through a colander, catching all of the stock in a bowl below.

continued overleaf

Variations and additions

- This can take a good amount of black pepper, so be generous if you like the flavour.
- Add some parsley to the meat mixture.

Pick the meat from the oxtail and shred the shin meat, discarding all the bones and any pieces of meat that seem dry. Place the meat in a large bowl along with the vegetables and mix to combine, then set aside.

Chill the stock until the fat rises to the top: this will take a few hours in the fridge, or if you're short on time, you can speed things up by putting it in the freezer. Remove the fat from the top and discard. Put the jellified stock in a saucepan over a low heat. Once liquid again, increase the heat to medium and bring to the boil, then reduce the heat to low and simmer until reduced by half, skimming off any impurities that float to the surface. Leave to cool, then pour onto the shredded meat and vegetables. Stir to combine, trying not to compact the mixture.

Fill the pre-baked pastry case almost to the top with the beef mixture, then level off with a palette knife. Top with your decorative pastry lid of choice and bake, according to the instructions on page 17.

Where my preference is to serve this pie hot, it is delicious cold too. If serving hot allow to cool for 5 minutes before slicing.

William Morris Inspired Leaves & Flowers

First, roll out a pastry platform and mark out your working area (see page 14). To make the thicker branch, hand-roll a strip of pastry. The thinner branches were made using the spaghetti cutter on a pasta machine. The leaves to the right were made using a pointed daisy cutter, cutting off the individual petals, and a small tear-shaped cutter was used for the leaves to the left. Use the back of a knife to score veins onto the leaves. For the flowers, use a daisy push cutter, then place a small ball of pastry in the centre of each. Arrange these on your pastry platform as you wish. You may want to use egg wash to glue the decorations in place; however, with more free-flowing designs like this, I tend not to, in case I want to move things.

Dogwood Flowers

Sometimes, nature's beauty can strike me unexpectedly, especially in plants or flowers. Now that I see the beauty in most things, I can't believe how I was so blind to it before, when my world was grey. There is a dogwood tree in a courtyard of a museum in Carlisle; a tree I had walked past countless times before, never even noticing it. The day I saw it properly for the first time, I was stopped in my tracks by the sight. This huge tree, absolutely covered in pink flowers, actually brought a tear to my eye. I feel emotional just thinking of that moment, as it was then that I realised I was finally awake, and open again to how beautiful life could be. It was quite the pivotal moment.

Search online for some flower and leaf templates, then print and cut them out to use as a guide for cutting out shapes from rolled-out pastry. Cut some thin strips for the branches; you can either use the tagliatelle cutter on a pasta machine, or hand-cut them using a pizza wheel. Lay the strips, flowers and leaf shapes decoratively across a pastry platform with a marked-out working area (see page 14). Finish the flowers with small circular cut-outs and emphasize each with thin strips of pastry placed around the outside of each and in the centre of the petals. The thin strips can be made using the spaghetti cutter on a pasta machine. Lastly, use the back of a knife to score the veins on each leaf.

Cod & Chorizo Pie

**Makes 1 large pie
or 6 small pies**

For the pastry

At least 2 batches savoury shortcrust pastry (page 11)

For the filling

1 red pepper

2 tablespoons plain flour

250g (9oz) skinless cod loin, cut into 3cm (1¼in) chunks

2 tablespoons olive oil for frying, plus extra for drizzling

100g (3½oz) cooking chorizo, skin removed, chopped

2 banana shallots, sliced, 150g (5½oz) prepped weight

2 fat garlic cloves, finely sliced

1 teaspoon smoked hot paprika

200g (7oz) finely chopped tomatoes

80g (3oz) canned or jarred butter beans, drained

100g (3½oz) cream cheese

small bunch of flat-leaf parsley, chopped

juice of ½ lemon

sea salt flakes and freshly ground black pepper

Variations and additions

• Swap the cod for monkfish or prepared tiger prawns.

Try to use a nice, thick piece of cod loin for this pie: large chunks of fish are needed, so they don't overcook before the pastry top is crisp. The addition of chorizo is wonderful; it adds a rich smokiness and mouth-watering depth of flavour. Truly delicious.

Line your tin with one batch of the pastry and blind-bake and trim according to the instructions on page 13. Leave the baked pastry case in the tin for filling and finishing.

First, char the pepper by either setting on the open flame of a gas hob, turning until all of the skin is blackened. Alternatively, use a culinary blowtorch or place in a hot oven and roast whole, for 45 minutes, turning halfway. When all blackened, wrap in clingfilm while hot and allow to sweat for 20 minutes. Remove the clingfilm, rinse under the tap and the skin will come off easily. The charred flavour will remain. Half, deseed and chop the pepper flesh and set to one side.

Scatter the flour over a large plate and sprinkle with plenty of salt and pepper. Toss the chunks of cod in the seasoned flour, coating well on all sides.

Heat a large frying pan over a high heat and add a thin layer of oil. Fry the fish chunks very quickly (perhaps for 20 seconds on each side), then remove from the pan onto a plate. Reduce the heat to low and add a little more oil to the pan, followed by the chorizo. Slowly fry for 10 minutes, allowing the wonderful fat to render and seep into the pan. Toss occasionally. Add the shallots, garlic and red pepper, along with the paprika, and season with some salt and pepper. Sauté for 5 minutes until softened. Add the tomatoes and simmer for 15 minutes until thickened slightly, then fold through the butter beans.

Loosen the cream cheese by beating it in a bowl, then stir this into the tomato mixture, along with the parsley and lemon juice. Check for seasoning, balancing the flavours to your taste. Allow to cool, then add the cod, stirring through gently so as not to break it up.

Fill the pre-baked pastry case almost to the top with the filling and level off with a palette knife. Top with your decorative pastry lid of choice and bake, according to the instructions on page 17.

This pie is best served hot, but do allow it 5 minutes before slicing.

Spirals

These spirals require lots of long, thin strips of pastry, which can be made using the spaghetti cutter on a pasta machine. The longer the strips, the fewer joins you will have. Roll out a pastry platform, and mark out your working area (see page 14), then find the centre point within that area. Using egg wash as a glue, brush a small area in the centre. Take 1 strip of pastry and curl the end into a tight spiral. Lay this upon the centre point. Coil the strip around, continuing with other strips until the edge of the marked area has been reached.

Victorian Floor

I have this thing with floors. I even follow an Instagram account of that very name: @ihavethisthingwithfloors. There is so much inspiration to be found in beautifully tiled floors, especially if you like a more geometric finish.

Roll out a pastry platform, and mark out your working area (see page 14). To make the pastry tiles, consistently rolled-out pastry is key. To achieve this, first hand-roll the pastry, then cut it into wide strips. Pass these strips through the plain roller of a pasta machine, set to the widest setting. Now cut the pastry into squares, using a ruler and pizza wheel. To make the triangles, cut some of the squares diagonally into halves or quarters. If you like, you can use edible paint to colour the pastry tiles in the colours of your choice. Allow to dry, then brush the pastry platform with egg wash and place the tiles in position, working up to and slightly over the edge of the marked-out working area. You can neaten this off when you transfer the lid to the pie. If you like, you can cover the joins using thin strips of pastry cut using the spaghetti cutter. See page 165 for the full design.

Antique Ring

When I look at this design now, it looks like it might have been inspired by something from a sci-fi movie. It was, in fact, based on an art deco ring I was admiring in the window of an antiques shop. The triangular shape and unusual setting of the stones caught my attention. The design and the expertise needed to make such an object made me pause to reflect for a while before walking on.

This design looks more complex than it really is. After rolling out the pastry platform and marking your working area (see page 14), measure out a square, set on the diagonal. The pattern is made up of strips of pastry cut using the tagliatelle and spaghetti cutters of a pasta machine. Within the borders and lines, rectangles and circles make up the rest of the design; these are made using cutters. The central spirals can be made using pastry spaghetti. Gently brush some egg wash onto the pastry platform to hold everything in place.

Vegetables

POTATO

Curried Potato Pie

**Makes 1 large pie
or 6 small pies**

For the pastry

At least 2 batches savoury
shortcrust pastry (page 11)

For the filling

2 x 400ml (14oz) cans
coconut milk

400g (14oz) waxy potatoes,
sliced to 0.5cm (½in) thick

1 tablespoons olive oil

1 onion, very finely chopped,
125g (4½oz) prepped weight

2 fat garlic cloves, finely
grated

½ teaspoon cumin seeds

½ teaspoon ground
fenugreek

½ teaspoon freshly ground
black pepper

1 teaspoon garam masala

1 teaspoon curry powder,
mild, medium or hot
according to preference

1–2 hot green chillies,
deseeded and finely
chopped

2 spring onions, finely sliced

handful of coriander leaves,
finely chopped

juice of ½ lemon, or to taste

sea salt flakes

Potatoes are a true kitchen staple: versatile, comforting and always readily available. They are the perfect 'sponge' ingredient, soaking up and carrying all kinds of flavour without losing their own soothing charm. Play around with what you have in your cupboards and fridge if you want to enhance this base recipe. The heat in the filling can be taken up a few notches with extra chilli and spice.

Line your tin with one batch of the pastry and blind-bake and trim according to the instructions on page 13. Leave the baked pastry case in the tin for filling and finishing.

Give the coconut milk a good whisk to loosen, then place in a large saucepan with some salt and the sliced potatoes over a medium heat. Bring to a simmer and cook for 8–10 minutes or until tender. Drain, reserving the coconut milk, and allow the potatoes to steam dry.

Heat the oil in a frying pan over a medium heat. Add the onion and sauté with a sprinkling of salt for a couple of minutes, then add the garlic, cumin seeds, black pepper, garam masala, curry powder and chilli(es). Fry gently stirring all the while, until the spices are aromatic and the garlic and chilli have softened. Add 100ml (3½fl oz) of the reserved coconut milk to the pan. Stir well and simmer for a couple of minutes to reduce and thicken. Add the potatoes, stirring to coat them with the spiced sauce. Transfer to a bowl, then stir in the spring onions and coriander, along with lemon juice to taste. Add more salt if needed, then leave to cool completely.

Top with your decorative pastry lid of choice and bake, according to the instructions on page 17.

William Morris

There are a few designs within these pages that were inspired by the genius of textile designer William Morris. His patterns and artwork captivate me, and he was also a great poet. Oh, to be in the mind of such a creative person just for one day!

First roll out a pastry platform and mark out the working area using the tin being used (see page 14). Make the thin strips of the branches by passing rolled pastry through the spaghetti cutter of a pasta machine. Place them randomly in varying directions. Cut the leaves using both leaf and daisy push cutters with the individual petals cut and turned into leaf shapes. Indent each leaf with the back of a knife. Make the flowers with a daisy cutter. Once everything is in place, cut circles to form the centres, going all the way through the pastry platform too.

Sparks

Simple designs can be very eye-catching, like this one. Using two sizes of the same shaped cutter can be effective, as I did here with a rhombus cutter. I then cut circles directly from the pie lid using the small end of a piping nozzle. The cut-out circles were then added back to the design.

Graphic Floor Tiles

Highly graphic and geometric designs are very striking and much quicker to achieve than freestyle ones. What is important for a slick finish is accurate measurements and placement of the pieces. Measure and cut pastry tiles from rolled-out pastry (I would pass this through the plain roller of a pasta machine before cutting). Lay the squares onto a pastry platform with the working area marked out using the tin being used. Egg wash will hold the tiles in place. Use the edge of a ruler, perhaps, to space the tiles consistently. You could use small discs or other shapes in the cross sections to complete the look.

Crescent Necklace

My younger sons have been learning about the ancient Egyptians at school recently, and I've really enjoyed helping them with it. Years ago, I visited Cairo, on a two-day trip over from Cyprus: it was the most seasickness-inducing ferry crossing you can imagine. While I will never forget that boat ride, my short time in Egypt also made a lasting impression, as did the Tutankhamun exhibition we visited when there. My memories of Cairo prompted an online search, which led me to Egyptian jewellery. This pie top was inspired by some of the necklaces of that ancient time.

My favourite designs are those that just evolve as you go, building a pattern with no plan, using the cutters that are spread out across the desk and simply going with it. This was one of those. First, I marked out a crescent on a pastry platform, and laid little discs upon it, the rest is just a mixture of shapes using push and small metal cutters.

Roasted Pepper & Tomato Pies

Makes 6 small pies or tarts or 1 large pie or tart

For the pastry

At least 2 batches savoury shortcrust pastry (page 11)

For the filling

6 peppers, mixed colours if possible, halved and deseeded

4 fat garlic cloves, skin on, slightly bashed

6 large banana shallots, skin on, halved lengthways

100ml (3½fl oz) olive oil

2 rosemary sprigs

200g (7oz) baby plum tomatoes, halved

1 teaspoon dried oregano, plus extra to taste

150g (5½oz) feta, finely crumbled

50g (1¾oz) capers, rinsed

dried chilli flakes, to taste (optional)

juice of 1 lemon, to taste (optional)

sea salt flakes and freshly ground black pepper

The simple act of roasting most vegetables will enhance their flavour in the most delicious way, and this is especially true of tomatoes and peppers: the sweetness of both is amplified, making them distinctly moreish. I like to add capers, olives and lots of herbs to help channel a strong Mediterranean vibe. This pie is perfect served with a bitter leaf salad, dressed with a mouth-puckering vinegar.

Line six individual tins with one batch of the pastry and blind-bake and trim according to the instructions on page 13. Leave the baked pastry cases in the tins for filling and finishing.

Preheat the oven to 220°C/200°C fan/425°F/gas mark 7.

Lay the halved peppers side by side, cut side up, in a large roasting tray, then tuck the garlic and shallots in and around them, drizzling over half the oil. Add the rosemary sprigs and season with salt and pepper.

Arrange the tomatoes in a small roasting tray, cut side up; they need fit quite snugly so they don't burn. Drizzle with the remaining oil, then sprinkle with oregano and some salt. Put both trays in the oven. The peppers will take around 45 minutes to soften and char slightly, and the tomatoes around 30 minutes, so they will need to come out sooner – but do keep an eye on both trays. Give the peppers a good stir halfway through. Once roasted, set aside to cool.

When the peppers are cool enough to handle, chop them roughly and transfer to a bowl. Remove the shallots from their skins and add those to the bowl too, discarding any overly charred bits. Squeeze the softened garlic flesh from its skin and add to the bowl, along with the roasted tomatoes. There will be a lot of flavour in both roasting tins, so do utilize it. Scrape out any sticky bits and pour all of the delicious roasting oil into the bowl.

Add the feta and capers and toss to combine. Taste to check for balance of flavours. Add an extra sprinkling of oregano if needed. You may like to include a little more black pepper, or perhaps a pinch of chilli flakes if that's your thing. Some lemon juice will sharpen things up if that suits your taste.

continued overleaf

Variations and additions

- Add lemon zest to the pastry.
- Use different herbs, such as thyme or marjoram.
- Add olives or cooked aubergine to the vegetable mixture.
- Swap the feta for some cooked and sliced salad potatoes.

Once you're happy, fill the pre-baked pastry cases with the pepper mix and level off the surface using a palette knife. Top with your decorative pastry lids of choice and bake, according to the instructions on page 17.

These pies are delicious served either hot or cold. If serving hot, allow to cool for 5 minutes before eating.

ROASTED PEPPER & TOMATO TART

This filling also works well as a tart, and using different-coloured peppers is a great way to make it look extra-appetizing and beautiful.

Simply line six individual tins with one batch of savoury shortcrust pastry (page 11) and blind-bake and trim according to the instructions on page 13. Leave the baked pastry cases in the tins for filling and finishing. Any excess pastry can be used for decoration.

Follow the filling method as above, but only roast two of the peppers. While the tomatoes and peppers are roasting, chop the other peppers. Simply cutting them into small cubes looks great, but if you like, you can use a small shaped cutter for an extra bit of interest: I used a tear-shaped cutter for the small tarts pictured opposite.

Fill the pre-baked pastry cases with the roasted pepper and tomato mixture as above, and level off the surface using a palette knife. Top with the cut peppers, arranging them decoratively. Bake at 200°C/180°C fan/400°F/gas mark 6 for 35 minutes, or until the cut peppers on top are softened and starting to colour. The filling will be warmed through and delicious.

Pepper Petals & Pastry Leaves

The pepper petals were cut from the peppers using a tear-shaped metal cutter, but a similar result could be achieved by hand cutting into diamond shapes. The parsley pastry garnishes were made by using an online template, cutting around it to make the leaf shape. These were baked separately at 200°C/180°C fan/400°F/gas mark 6 for 10 minutes before being added to the cooked tarts.

Fern Fronds

Every year, a line of fern fronds would grow along the sandstone wall of my old house. I saw them as a nuisance. If I still lived there now, I would welcome the sight of them growing, and enjoy the way the shoots turned into coils of green before magically uncurling into these beautiful leaves. I suppose the inspiration here, as well as the leaves themselves, is acceptance: seeing and appreciating life through a different lens.

Recreate lifelike ferns by printing off a template found online. Cut the individual leaves from the paper then, using them as a guide, cut out the shapes from rolled pastry. Use the end of a wooden skewer to knock in the grooves and score the leaves. Cut stems by passing rolled pastry through the spaghetti cutter of a pasta machine. Lay the fern onto pastry platforms, working within a marked-out area (see page 14). The green paint (see page 174) is edible. Simply brush on using an artist's brush.

Paisley

I love a pie top that requires this amount of patience, cutting lots of small shapes and placing them with care, the actions becoming meditative. The shapes were cut using push cutters and to ensure they were all the same depth the pastry was first rolled through the plain roller of a pasta machine, set to the widest setting. Gently score the lines and teardrop shapes on to a pastry platform then place the small shapes along those lines. A small amount of egg wash will keep all the shapes in place. If you find it tricky to place the small shapes, a cocktail stick may help.

Asparagus, Broad Bean & Pea Pie

**Makes 1 large pie
or 6 small pies**

For the pastry

At least 2 batches savoury
shortcrust pastry (page 11)

For the filling

50g (1¾oz) butter

1 fat garlic clove, finely
grated

zest and juice of ½ lemon

6 thick asparagus spears,
trimmed and chopped into
2cm (¾in) pieces

180g (6.5oz) broad beans,
blanched and skins
removed

175g (6oz) frozen petit pois,
defrosted

small bunch of dill, tarragon,
chervil or flat-leaf parsley,
finely chopped

100g (3½oz) ricotta

2 teaspoons Dijon mustard
(optional)

75ml (2½fl oz) double cream

1 beaten egg

sea salt flakes and freshly
ground black pepper

Just looking at a plate full of greenery can make you feel better, and the gorgeous emerald hues of these spring vegetables make for a truly beautiful and appetizing meal. I like to give the asparagus, beans and peas a flavour-boosting head start before they are submerged in their savoury ricotta bath – everything benefits from being swamped in brown butter in my opinion, and these springtime treasures are no exception.

I always remove the rubbery skins from the broad beans, revealing the vivid green bean underneath, but this isn't essential, so you can skip it if you wish.

Line your tin with the pastry and blind-bake and trim according to the instructions on page 13. Leave the baked pastry case in the tin for filling and finishing. Any excess pastry can be used for decorations.

Melt the butter in a small sauté pan over a medium heat until it starts to foam and the aroma changes to one of nutty deliciousness. Add the garlic and lemon zest and season with salt and pepper, then toss in the asparagus, broad beans and peas. Jiggle the pan so the butter coats everything well, then gently cook for a couple of minutes. The asparagus should be tender if pricked with the point of a knife. Add the lemon juice and toss through, then transfer the mixture to a bowl to cool, making sure to scrape out every drop of the tasty butter. Once cool, stir in the herbs. Taste, then add a little more salt, lemon juice or herbs if needed.

Beat the ricotta for a couple of minutes until smooth, then stir in the mustard, if using, followed by the cream. Don't be tempted to whisk too much at this stage, or the cream will thicken. Add the beaten egg and combine.

Cover the base of the pre-baked pastry case with the buttery vegetables and pour over the ricotta mixture.

continued overleaf

Variations and additions

- Add lemon zest to the pastry.

- Add ground nutmeg to the ricotta mixture.

- Stir a handful of watercress or spinach into the vegetable mixture.

- Experiment with different vegetables.

Top with your decorative pastry lid of choice and bake, according to the instructions on page 17.

Serve hot or cold, with a handful of watercress and a lemon wedge on the side.

Peacock Mandala *(page 180)*

As the green filling of this pie was so bright and appealing, I thought it would be nice to show it off rather than cover it with pastry. Cut-out shapes achieve that perfectly. Lay the design upon a pastry platform working within a marked-out area (see page 14). Start by making a flower shape off-centre using 8 tear-shaped pastry pieces. Then work outwards, building up your design using cut-out pastry shapes a layer at a time. When the pattern is complete, transfer it to the fridge to chill for about 30 minutes. Then cut the holes through the design and platform using metal cutters. It is important to chill the pastry well so that the pieces can be removed easily.

Textiles *(opposite)*

Patience required! Lots of small shapes were used here, cut using push cutters. I gave my kids that job, which they enjoyed. I suggest passing rolled pastry through the plain roller of a pasta machine, set to the widest setting first, so each will be the same depth. Roll out a pastry platform and mark the working area with the tin being used (see page 14). Carefully lay the small shapes around different-sized discs, a small amount of egg wash will keep them in place. If you find it tricky to place the small shapes, use a cocktail stick. The leaf shapes were cut using a tear-shaped cutter, then scored with the back of a knife.

Vegetable Pies

**Makes 1 large pie
or 6 small pies**

This excellent fridge-raid pie is a great way to use up any random vegetables you may have around. Of course, you can go out and buy fresh veg for this too. There really are no rules on what to use: you know the vegetables you like best, and which ones work well with each other. I've used a bechamel sauce to bind everything together, spiked with mustard, herbs and plenty of pepper.

For the pastry

At least 2 batches savoury shortcrust pastry (page 11)

Line six individual tins with one batch of the pastry and blind-bake and trim according to the instructions on page 13. Leave the baked pastry cases in the tin for filling and finishing.

For the filling

600g (1lb 5oz) mixed vegetables, such as carrots, courgettes, aubergines, beetroots, potatoes, peas, peeled if necessary and cut in 1cm (½in) cubes

1 tablespoon olive oil for sautéing

½ teaspoon caraway seeds (optional)

50g (1¾oz) salted butter

25g (1oz) plain flour

250ml (9fl oz) milk or vegetable stock

1 tablespoon wholegrain mustard (optional)

bunch of soft herbs of your choice, finely chopped (optional)

sea salt flakes and freshly ground black pepper

Begin by preparing the vegetables. This will depend on what you are using. Root vegetables or any long beans will need to be simmered until tender in a pan of well-salted water, then drained. Softer-fleshed vegetables, such as peas, courgettes and aubergines should be sautéed in a frying pan with the oil, caraway seeds (if using) and some salt and pepper until tender. Drain well on a plate lined with kitchen paper. Set all the vegetables aside while you make the binding sauce.

Melt the butter in a saucepan over a medium heat. Add the flour and allow to sizzle for a minute or two, stirring continuously. Add half the milk or stock and whisk until smooth, then add the remainder. Continue to whisk until smooth, then simmer gently until the sauce thickens. Add the mustard, if using. Allow to cool, then fold through the herbs.

Add the cooled vegetables to the sauce and mix well. Taste and adjust the seasoning if needed: you might choose to add more mustard, salt or herbs. Fill the pre-baked pastry cases with the mixture, then top with your decorative pastry lids of choice and bake, according to the instructions on page 17.

Serve hot or cold, however hot is my personal preference.

Variations and additions

- Swap the caraway seeds for fennel seeds, ground nutmeg or other favourite spices.

- Add cheese to the binding sauce.

- Add some poached chicken for a meaty version of this pie.

Bleeding Hearts

Another interpretation of emotion. The bleeding heart flower is not the actual inspiration here; I just used it as a visual metaphor for my feelings at the time of making. I think creative people are naturally emotional – I certainly am. If I feel something, I really feel it, so much so that in years past, I learned to suppress my emotions as a defence mechanism. Eventually, this tactic made me become emotionally numb, which I now know is not a healthy way to deal with painful emotions. Now I do feel again, I know it is far better to feel, even if it's painful: embrace all emotions, good and bad, and express them.

The flower buds of the bleeding hearts are made using heart push cutters, with the heart shapes then opened at the bottom. The larger leaves are made using a tear-shaped cutter and the smaller ones using a pointed daisy cutter, the individual petals then cut off. The leaves are shaped by taking little nicks of pastry from each side and scored down the middle. The thin stems were made by passing rolled pastry through the spaghetti cutter on a pasta machine. Assemble on a pastry platform, and work within a marked-out area (see page 14). The design can be glued into place using egg wash.

Lotus Flowers

A design perhaps for when time is short but an effective finish is still desired. Roll out a pastry platform and mark out the working area using the tin being used (see page 14). Cut thin strips using the spaghetti cutter on a pasta machine then lay on a diagonal using a ruler as guide for equal spacing. The flower heads are made using tear-shaped cutters, the petals fanned out and laid in position. Small circular cut-outs (I use the end of a piping nozzle) can then be added as extra details.

Vegetable Ribbon Tart

**Makes 1 large tart
or 6 small tarts**

For the pastry

1 batch savoury shortcrust
pastry (page 11)

For the filling

250g (9oz) Maris Piper or
King Edward potatoes,
peeled and cut into 5cm
(2in) chunks

200g (7oz) salted butter

100ml (3½fl oz) double
cream

large handful of soft herbs
of your choice, such as
parsley, chervil, dill, basil or
tarragon, plus extra to serve
if desired

1.5kg (3lb 5oz) selection
of vegetables for
ribboning (I used carrot,
swede, beetroot, potato
and courgette) – extra
vegetables are needed to
achieve enough ribbons,
any leftovers may be used in
other dishes

1 teaspoon fennel seeds
(optional)

These tarts are fun, funky and colourful: a real show-stopping way to use
vegetables. Even the most committed vegetable-dodging child will want a slice,
I'm sure. The vegetables can be changed to suit the season, and if you like you could
just use one type of vegetable to concentrate on a particular flavour. It's easy to
let style take over from substance here, so do pack as much flavour into the mash as
possible, and season the blanching water well for the vegetable ribbons. Brushing a
browned butter (see page 99) over the finished tart will also help, as will a finishing
salt, some toasted spices, or a scattering of herbs and interesting edible leaves.

You'll need a specialist tool to shave the vegetables into ribbons. I use
the vegetable sheet attachment on my KitchenAid. The fatter the vegetable, the
easier it will be to shave into ribbons, so bear this in mind when you're shopping.

Line your tin with the pastry and blind-bake and trim according to the instructions
on page 13. Leave the baked pastry case in the tin for filling and finishing. Any
excess pastry can be used for decoration.

Place the potato chunks in a large pan of well-salted water and simmer for 15
minutes or until soft. Drain, then mash (I use a potato ricer). Stir in half the butter,
along with the cream. Season to taste with salt and pepper. Leave to cool, then stir
through the chopped herbs and set aside.

Prepare the vegetable ribbons following the instructions provided with your cutter.
Do try and choose the largest vegetables of your chosen variety, as this will give you
longer ribbons for curling or shaping.

Apart from the courgette, the vegetable ribbons will all need to be blanched, but
the different varieties will not all cook and soften in the same time, so you'll need
to blanch each one separately. Bring a large pan of well-salted water to a simmer,
and have a bowl of cold or iced water ready. Blanch the vegetable ribbons by type
until just softened, but not starting to break up. Keep checking to see when they're
ready. When done, lift the ribbons out of their pan using a slotted spoon or tongs
and plunge into the cold water. Continue until all the ribbons are ready. If you're
using beetroot, do this last so the colour that leaches into the water doesn't stain
any other vegetables being blanched. Once all the vegetable ribbons have been
blanched and refreshed in the cold water, dry them with clean tea towels (again
treating the beetroot last, if using).

continued overleaf

Variations and additions

- Swap the fennel seeds for another spice: cumin seeds, star anise, or crushed coriander seeds would all work. You could even add some ground spices or your favourite curry blend. Go bold and add plenty of flavour.

- Add some cheese to the mashed potatoes.

When you're ready to assemble, preheat the oven to 200°C/180°C fan/400°F/gas mark 6. Fill the pre-baked pastry case with the mashed potato and smooth over with the back of a spoon. Use the vegetable ribbons to cover the surface of the mash, either by curling them into spirals or laying them side by side, as shown on pages 189 and 191. Alternatively, you can create something new: just start by rolling, swirling and placing and see what appears!

Melt the remaining butter in a saucepan over a medium heat and warm until it starts to foam and smells nutty. Remove from the heat, pass through a metal sieve and allow to cool a little, then add the fennel seeds to infuse.

Brush the surface of the tart with plenty of the flavoured butter, then sprinkle over some salt flakes. Cover loosely with foil and bake for 30 minutes, or until the tart is hot. Serve straight away, using a super-sharp knife to slice.

Vegetable Ribbons – Straight

The vegetables themselves were the inspiration here: when you have ingredients as colourful and beautiful as these, that's all you need. When styling the two ribbon tarts, I had no prior plan: it was just a case of seeing what sprang to mind when I started. I particularly love this one, as I think the finish looks almost like fabric.

The instructions on how to cook and blanch the vegetable ribbons are in the recipe method. The ribbons may need trimming, so that they are all the same width. When ready to lay the ribbons, select the variety of vegetable ribbons at random and layer up say ten at a time. Place on the potato and trim to size using a sharp knife. Repeat until the surface is covered.

Vegetable Ribbons – Curls *(above and overleaf)*

The instructions on how to cook and blanch the vegetable ribbons are in the recipe method. The ribbons may need trimming, so that they are all the same width. When curling into spirals either select one vegetable type or two for a multicoloured swirl. Mix the sizes of the spirals to create a pleasing, non-uniform and colourful finish.

Mushroom & Onion Pie

**Makes 1 large pie
or 6 small pies**

For the pastry

At least 2 batches savoury
shortcrust pastry (page 11)

For the filling

250g (9oz) banana shallots,
skin on, halved lengthways

100ml (3½fl oz) olive oil

60g (2¼oz) salted butter

250g (9oz) chestnut
mushrooms, finely sliced

250g (9oz) field mushrooms,
finely sliced

250g (9oz) button
mushrooms, left whole

2 large garlic cloves, very
finely chopped

1 tablespoon freshly
chopped thyme leaves

1 tablespoon freshly
chopped flat-leaf parsley

sea salt flakes and freshly
ground pepper

For the sauce

50g (1¾oz) salted butter

25g (1oz) plain flour

250ml (9fl oz) milk or
mushroom/vegetable stock

2 tablespoons wholegrain
mustard (optional)

This is such a great vegetarian pie filling, and absolutely packed with umami flavour. It can be adapted easily: the addition of a melting cheese, would be fantastic idea; or, if you wanted some meat, perhaps try including some crispy fried cubes of pancetta.

Line your tin with one batch of the pastry and blind-bake and trim according to the instructions on page 13. Leave the baked pastry case in the tin for filling and finishing.

Preheat the oven to 200°C/180°C fan/400°F/gas mark 6.

Select a suitable-sized roasting tray that will fit the shallots snugly – if there is too much space around them, they can burn. Arrange the shallots in the tray cut-side up. Drizzle 3 tablespoons of the olive oil, sprinkle well with salt and pepper, and roast for 45 minutes, stirring every so often. You are aiming for meltingly soft shallot petals that have just a little charring. Leaving on the skins will prevent burning. When done, remove from the oven and leave to cool in the tray.

Heat the butter and 2 tablespoons of the olive oil in a large frying pan over a medium heat. Add all of the fresh mushrooms, season with a good pinch of salt and pepper, and cook for 20 minutes, stirring every so often. After this time, the mushrooms will have released most of their moisture and will start to fry.

Add the garlic, thyme and the remaining oil. Cook for a further 5 minutes, stirring occasionally. Transfer the mushroom mixture to a large bowl and leave to cool, then stir in the parsley.

Remove the skins from the shallots and discard. Add the softened flesh to the mushrooms.

To make the sauce, melt the butter in a saucepan over a medium heat. Add the flour and allow to sizzle for 1 minute, stirring continuously. Add half the milk (or stock) and whisk until smooth, then add the remainder. Continue to whisk until smooth, then simmer gently until the sauce thickens. Add the mustard, if using. Pour the sauce over the mushroom and shallot mixture and gently fold everything together. Leave to cool fully.

Fill the pre-baked pastry case with the mushroom filling and level off the surface. Top with your decorative pastry lid of choice and bake, according to the instructions on page 17.

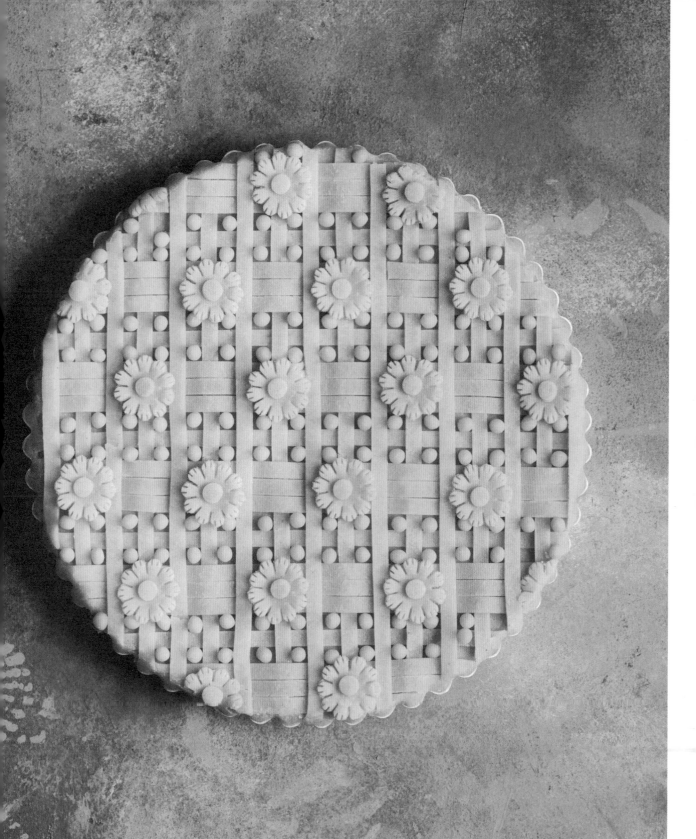

Basket Weave with Flowers

Start by rolling a pastry platform and mark out the working area (see page 14). Cut plenty of strips for the lattice, by first rolling pastry by hand. Cut that into wide strips and pass through the plain roller on a pasta machine, set to the widest setting. Finally pass through the tagliatelle cutter. Lay the strips side by side across the surface of the pastry platform. When done count three strips then remove one, leave one then remove another and repeat. The savoury shortcrust used to create this weave can crack easily so I suggest you start to weave from halfway down, then when the bottom is reached, turn the paper the pastry platform is resting on and weave the remaining half. To do this, lay a ruler horizontally across the strips halfway down then lift each section of three strips and rest over the ruler. Leave a space, then lay a strip horizontally across the remaining strips. Replace the sets of three. Leave a space then lay another strip horizontally across the top. Repeat the process of lifting and replacing the sets of three strips until all of the strips have been woven.

The daisies were cut using carnation cutters. To use these successfully the pastry must be chilled sufficiently. Lay the flowers on the cross sections of the weave, topping each with a disc of pastry. Fill the gaps between the basket weave with four small balls. A little egg wash will hold them in place. To size the pastry balls consistently, use a small push cutter for each, rolling the pastry into balls in the palm of your hand. See page 195 for the entire, unbaked design.

William Morris Bay

Another pie lid inspired by one of my favourite designers, William Morris. This is my take on his bay leaf embroidery design for a cushion, the original of which is part of the collection in the Victoria and Albert Museum in London; I have added it to my visit wish list. I first discovered this pattern in a textile book, randomly selected from a shelf in my local library.

Aubergine Curry Pie

**Makes 1 large pie
or 6 small pies**

This curry is simple – deliciously so. Add extra heat if that's what you like, or use your favourite spice blends.

For the pastry

At least 2 batches savoury shortcrust pastry (page 11)

Line your tin with one batch of the pastry and blind-bake and trim according to the instructions on page 13. Leave the baked pastry case in the tin for filling and finishing.

For the filling

3 tablespoons olive oil

1 medium onion, peeled and chopped into 1cm (½in) dice

1 aubergine, chopped into 2cm (¾in) chunks, 200g (7oz) prepped weight

1 green pepper, chopped into 2cm (¾in) chunks

2 garlic cloves, finely sliced

5cm (2in) piece of fresh ginger, finely chopped

1 red chilli, deseeded and finely chopped

1 teaspoon mild curry powder

1 teaspoon garam masala

1 teaspoon ground ginger

1 tablespoon ground fenugreek

2 large ripe tomatoes, chopped

200ml (7fl oz) coconut cream

handful of freshly chopped coriander

sea salt flakes

To make the filling, heat a large frying pan over a high heat until smoking. Add the oil, along with the onion, aubergines and peppers and a sprinkling of salt. Fry for 10 minutes, stirring often, until softened and taking on some colour. Reduce the heat to medium, then add the garlic, ginger and chilli. Fry for another minute before adding the spices. Stir well for 1–2 minutes, enjoying the aromas. Add the chopped tomatoes and coconut cream, then reduce the heat to low and simmer for 10 minutes until the curry thickens, then remove from the heat and leave to cool completely. Stir through the fresh coriander. Taste and adjust the seasoning if needed.

Fill the pre-baked pastry case with the curry mixture and level off the surface. Top with your decorative pastry lid of choice and bake, according to the instructions on page 17.

This pie is best enjoyed hot from the oven, but do allow it to sit for 5 minutes before slicing.

Large Daisy

Tear-shaped cutters are probably the most used shape throughout this book because the shape is very versatile, capable of making up a huge array of designs. Although this design is simplistic, I do think it is very elegant. Roll out a pastry platform and mark the working area (see page 14). Gently score the working area into squares, using the width of a ruler. Use the squares as a guide for laying the flower pattern. Use the tear-shaped cut-outs and circles to create the look.

Church Ceiling

*This design was inspired by the ceiling in Bath Cathedral, a truly spectacular sight.
When first I walked through those doors and looked up, I was overcome with emotion.
These moments stay with you. I sat for a while in silence, taking in the work of others
and the spiritual presence, lighting a candle for my mum and for Ged.*

Cut thin strips of pastry using the spaghetti cutter on a pasta machine. Cut small
daisies using a push cutter. Prepare the pastry platforms (see page 14). Use four strips
of pastry to section each platform into eight, then use four extra strips per eighth
to create the pattern. Add the daisies at the joins.

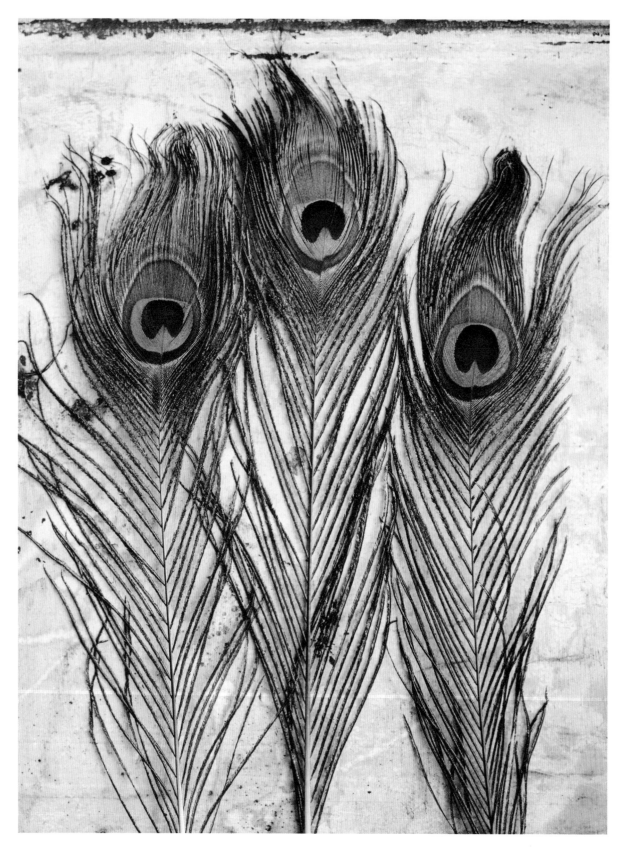

Oven-roasted Plum Tomato & Potato Pie

**Makes 1 large pie
or 6 small pies**

For the pastry

At least 2 batches savoury shortcrust pastry (page 11)

For the oven-roasted tomatoes

250g (9oz) plum tomatoes, halved

2 tablespoons of olive oil

1 teaspoon dried oregano

dried chilli flakes (optional)

sea salt flakes

For the filling

2 tablespoons olive oil

1 large onion, finely sliced, 200g (7oz) prepped weight

2 fat garlic cloves, finely sliced

1 tablespoon tomato purée

½ teaspoon dried chilli flakes (optional)

½ teaspoon dried oregano

200g (7oz) salad potatoes, chopped into 1cm (½in) cubes

50g (1¾oz) your favourite olives, stoned and quartered

50g (1¾oz) capers, rinsed

large handful of fresh basil leaves

sea salt flakes and freshly ground black pepper

I love the intensity of oven-roasted tomatoes: their flavour becomes so sweet and concentrated. When nestled among the potatoes in this pie filling, they give a burst of flavour and moisture like no other. If decent fresh tomatoes are in short supply, you could use shop-bought sun-dried tomatoes, or tubs of sun-blushed tomatoes instead.

Line your tin with one batch of the pastry and blind-bake and trim according to the instructions on page 13. Leave the baked pastry case in the tin for filling and finishing.

Preheat the oven to 220°C/200°C fan/425°F/gas mark 7.

Arrange the halved tomatoes in a roasting tray in which they fit snugly, positioning them cut-side up. Drizzle with the olive oil and sprinkle over the oregano and chilli flakes (if using), along with some salt. Roast for around 30 minutes until the tomatoes are softened and starting to collapse, and hopefully have some charring around the edges. Remove from the oven and leave to cool in the tray.

To make the filling, heat the oil in a large frying pan over a medium heat. Add the onion and a sprinkling of salt and pepper and cook for about 15 minutes until the onion softens and turns a light golden colour, stirring from time to time to prevent anything catching on the bottom of the pan.

Add the garlic and fry for 5 minutes more, then add the tomato purée, chilli flakes (if using) and oregano. Stir well and cook for a couple of minutes, then remove from the heat and leave to cool.

Boil the potato cubes in a pan of well-salted boiling water for about 8 minutes until they are softened but not collapsing. Drain and add them to the onion mixture. Allow to cool, then stir in the roasted tomatoes, scraping in every drop of the roasting juices from the tray. Toss through the olives and capers and add the basil. Check for seasoning, adjusting if needed.

Fill the pre-baked pastry case with the mixture and level off the surface. Top with your decorative pastry lid of choice and bake, according to the instructions on page 17.

Delicious served hot or cold.

Decorated Peacock Feather

A natural progression from the other pastry feathers featured in this book is the more elaborate and colourful peacock feather. When we styled and photographed this shot, Andrew and I were really excited by the visual. Personally, I feel that this is the shot of the book, a true expression of Art in Pastry. I'll remember the moment we captured this shot forever: two creative people, completely on the same wavelength, creating photographic magic.

Roll the pastry through a pasta machine, first through the plain roller (set to the widest setting) then through the spaghetti cutter. For the peacock feather shape, search online for feather templates and print your favourite. Cut this out and use as a template to cut feathers from rolled-out pastry. Lay the pastry feather upon a rolled-out pastry platform (see page 14). Brush the feather shape lightly with egg wash. Use the spaghetti strips first to lay the central spine down the middle of the feather then lay strips side by side on either side of the spine to replicate the feather strands. The strips needn't be measured, just lay them down, then pull to break at the right point. Add a second layer of strips, although not too many this time – just enough to create some 'movement' by placing the strands in slightly different directions. The eye of the feather was made by creating a spiral using the spaghetti pastry and small balls of pastry. I then lightly applied edible paint using an artist's brush. Metallic sprinkles complete the look.

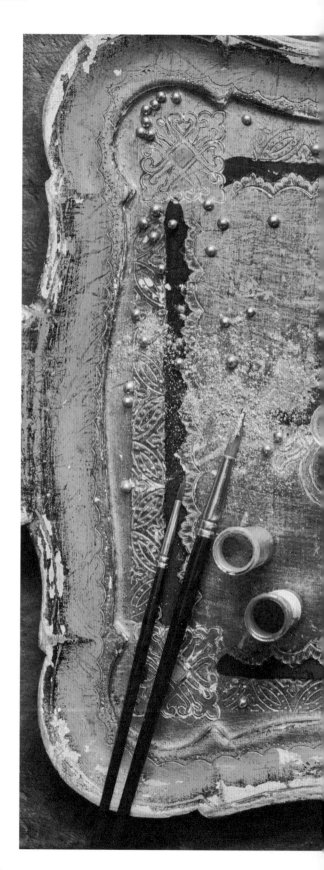

EQUIPMENT

Free-standing mixer: I use a KitchenAid and although it's an expensive piece of kitchen equipment, if you bake and cook a lot it will be worth it. As well as using it to make my pastry and fillings, I have a few of the attachments too, for example the pasta rollers and the vegetable sheet cutter, used to prepare the vegetable ribbons for the tarts on pages 189 and 192–3.

Bakeware: I have a wide selection of bakeware, primarily made by Silverwood. The quality and consistency of finish that their products bring to my baking is unquestionable. They will last a lifetime if cared for properly and will undoubtedly help to achieve the desired results. I use loose-bottomed tart tins for both tarts and pies when using shortcrust pastry. Baking sheets to rest your tins on in the oven are also essential.

Knives: A decent kitchen knife will be an investment and you will use it most days. I have a few knives but find myself reaching for the same two over and over. The first is a Japanese chef's knife and the other a small paring knife. Whatever your preference, keep them sharp, it will make all the difference. As well as sharp knives, palette knives are indispensable utensils, both straight and cranked, large and small, I even have a miniature palette knife which is great for tucking in stray pastry edges.

Mandoline: I use a Zyliss Swiss mandoline for preparing any finely sliced fruit or vegetables, I have found this the absolute best mandoline for the job as the blade will not move and has various blade options to experiment with.

Peeler: A Swiss-style swivel-headed vegetable peeler is the best tool for shaving pastry cases.

Measuring spoons: Don't use spoons from the cutlery drawer, they're not the same!

Pastry brushes: I use a variety of artist's brushes for adding colour or glitter or for use when egg-washing the pastry tops. The smaller brushes will allow an even brushing and won't displace any of the intricate detail.

Oven thermometer: Unless you really know your oven, I would get one. They're not expensive, and will aid the perfect bake, especially for the lemon, white chocolate and pumpkin tarts.

Rolling pin: A pin that feels right under your hand is what works best. I have recently started using a tapered pin and it is now by far my favourite.

Decorative cutters: I use a wide selection of cutters: small metal shapes, fancy biscuit cutters (as pictured here) and various plastic push cutters (designed for fondant icing). All can be easily found instore or online.

Non-stick baking paper: Great for rolling pastry between a couple of sheets.

Pasta machine: An essential piece of kit for rolling and cutting pastry for decorative work. If buying a hand-cranked machine, I can recommend an Imperia Classic as it is solid and feels sturdy while rolling, although cheaper machines will work too. If you have a KitchenAid or similar, the pasta-rolling attachments are a worthwhile investment.

Index

Acknowledgements

Starting right at the top with Jo Copestick, publisher at Kyle Books, for allowing so much creative freedom and providing never-ending encouragement and guidance. Next up, my creative soulmate Andrew Montgomery. It's safe to say we create magical pictures together, yet our food pictures are only amplified by the rest of your exceptional photographs. I love working with you, Andrew, truly the best shoot days ever. What a blast, what creativity, what a playlist. I shall never forget your commitment during that dahlia shot for as long as I live, AYE.

Rachel Cross, thanks again for another beautifully designed book, I can only imagine the chaos of trying to bring my ideas into a readable format. The book has captured the creative energy we were hoping for: thank you. A wider thank you to all at Kyle Books too, the unsung heroes who just make things happen, as well as Tara. I know this wasn't an easy book to edit, thanks for bringing it together in a sensical way! I hope you all love it as much as I do.

The shoot prep for this book was immense and when I called for help, my friends appeared without hesitation. You are all so very dear to me, I literally couldn't have managed with you. So, here's a special thanks to the prep and shoot massive. The two Nicky's – A & L – I love you both so much, you are truly the best, your help, energy and laughter will never be forgotten. The two Sarah's – H & T - new friends made through an Instagram request! It was amazing to have you on board. Sarah T, we must never forget the days Pamela was around, she was a right giggle. Emma, I loved our prep day together, thanks so much for your time. Vicki, pastry rolling machine! I bet you never want to see another pastry case as long as you live. Jeez we smashed the prep that day, didn't we? NO SURRENDER!! Sandra, never ever far away with a helping hand, whatever the request – you know I treasure our friendship. Jean, never-ending thank yous for the week's worth of school runs, you are a wonderful lady; I appreciate the help with the boys so much. Steven, thank you also for helping with the boys, for playing all the board games and for paying that taxi!

Moments never to forget. Isabel, you never failed to find us a solution for our random photography requests, from gardens to wellies and a kitchen... even a pond! Huge thanks to Rebecca of The Pretty Wild Flower Co., Instagram @theprettywildflowerco, and to Mike McNeil for providing the vast array of dahlias for the beautiful shot on pages 54–55. It was so very kind of you to do that for us, your flowers made for a very stunning photograph, I'm sure you'll agree. Jen at Cathedral Lodge Antiques, Carlisle, thank you for allowing us to rummage through your beautiful jewellery. Again, the shot on page 64 is one of true beauty and helps to tie the inspirations and the creations in this book together. Anita and Roy at www.carvetii-interiors.co.uk, thanks as always, for allowing me to work in your showroom – that green kitchen is the perfect workspace and studio. Special thanks to Rag Arts, www.ragarts.co.uk, for the stunning bespoke backgrounds. Art!

A wider thank you to each and every one of my friends, too many to name individually but you know who you are. You have supported me yet again throughout this process. It wasn't easy this time (never is), but moving twice and finalizing a divorce throughout...well, I only just managed to hold it together, and that was because of you all. I would have undoubtedly crumbled without you. A special mention goes to my two amigos, Justine and Richard. For keeping me belly laughing and on track during the last six months... for catching me just before a fall and for supporting me in everything, in every way... always. I love you both. Sesh needed!

Finally, thanks to my three boys, Evan, Oscar and Myles. Never stop creating, never stop shining, be unique always.

Here's to the next chapter...
Julie xx